WORKBOOK

FOR CANADIAN AND US INMATES, ADDICTS, ———— AND ————
COMMUNITY GROUPS

BY STEVE BRADLEY

Pauline,
Many thanks
— Steve Bradley
19/11/2024

Workbook For Canadian and US Inmates, Addicts, and Community Groups
Copyright © 2024 by Steve Bradley

tellwell

Tellwell Talent
www.tellwell.ca

ISBN
978-1-998190-11-9 (Paperback)

Name of Participant _____

Date _____

In Community or Corrections _____

Dedication

To the U.S. doctor and his team and the First Nations people who saved my life. Before God taught me to forgive myself, and my kidnapper.

Table of Contents

Foreword

I've known Steve Bradley since high school in Victoria, BC. We lived in the same neighborhood and became close friends. In 1972, I became a Christian and shared my faith with everyone I met, but for some reason, I never told Steve. I felt bad about this. Five years later I got a telephone call from my friend. He suggested we "get together" so I drove over to see him.

On the way I received a word from the Lord, "If you really want to know, it's Jesus!"

The first thing Steve asked me was, "What's happened to you?" He then described the differences he noticed in me. I replied, "If you really want to know, it's Jesus!" Steve asked, "How do I do it? What do I do?" At first, I didn't understand what he was saying. Then I realized he was asking me how to become a Christian. I then prayed with him to receive Jesus Christ. That Sunday we went to Trinity Christian Centre, and Steve was baptized.

After becoming a Christian, Steve encountered difficulties and returned to his life of crime and drugs. Steve had been locked up several times and in 1987 he was in Vancouver Island Regional Correctional Centre (VIRCC). While incarcerated, Steve recommitted his life to Jesus. He received God's call to help his fellow inmates. Steve began meetings in the prison, called Connection to Freedom, and when he was released continued these meetings in the form of a Christian support group for addicts and ex-offenders. These meetings were sustained for over twenty-five years at various venues such as the Mustard Seed Street Church, the Salvation Army Addictions Recovery Centre, VIRCC, Centennial United Church, the Manchester House, and the Needle Exchange as well as other locations.

Because Steve once lived a life of crime and drugs, prior to God's miraculous transformation of his life, he is well suited to bringing the message of hope and redemption through Jesus to addicts and ex-offenders and others who are suffering. Having worked with Steve in this ministry for many years, I see the challenge is to turn people off drugs and onto the Lord-from being addicted to substances to being addicted to the Lord and His Word. I thank the Lord for Steve's relentless desire to serve Christ with his new book for prisoners.

– Ross Pomeroy

Connection to Freedom

I can easily remember my first encounter with Steve Bradley. It was in jail. I was a correctional officer and Steve had been admitted to my unit— physically and mentally at the bottom. He was drug sick, alcohol sick and he appeared to have very little hope. He just seemed like a lost soul. Steve stayed in his cell for days, and I wondered if he would ever come around. Substance withdrawal was tearing at his mind and body.

Gradually, Steve found his feet and began to move about his cell and interact with other inmates. It was through one of these interactions that Steve made the decision to live.

Steve began working on a project that became known as Connection to Freedom. He took on this project with determination and dedication. He gained strength and a sense of purpose. At every opportunity, Steve spoke with others about Connection to Freedom and the project grew. I don't know how many inmates Steve Bradley helped, but the entire jail knew of him and his work.

Upon his release, Steve took the idea conceived in jail into the community. He continued to work with people with drug and alcohol problems through Connection to Freedom.

After all these years, Steve's name still comes up in my work. For the past eleven years, I have been working in the community in Adult Corrections. Now and then a client will mention that he is or has been involved with Connection to Freedom, and I remember Steve Bradley, the lost soul who was pulled up from the bottom. Steve continues to make an important contribution to the community through Connection to Freedom. – T. L, Adult Corrections.

I saw firsthand the creation of Connection to Freedom. Negative behaviour and boredom were ultimately replaced, letting inmates advance to worthwhile goals. I recommend Connection to Freedom to any correctional institution." – E.C., Correctional Officer, VIRCC.

The Workbook Program
and The Community

First and foremost, this workbook is history not present-day information. However, the exercises and of course God's word, are all present day. Because the book refers to Canada and the US, you will notice different spellings. The exercises in this workbook are from my own experiences which were a four pack a day cigarette addiction, 27 years active as an alcoholic, 18 years addicted to heroin, and other opioids. Through prayer and the Bible (Mark 11:25-26 NKJ) I gave up cigarettes, two years later, at a Prayer Group, taught by Rev Arthur Willis, at the Mustard Seed Street Church, the Lord took alcohol, heroin, and other opioids from my life. I live as the Bible says: "one day at a time".

My purpose in sharing this information is to make sure you understand that rehabilitation from behaviour that leads to crime, and recovery from addictions to alcohol and drugs, is the program. The beginning is formed to ease you into the opportunity to tell your story, write a poem, draw a picture. As you get further into the book, exercises become more difficult. But changing behavior is not easy. However, you will be taking the road to a better life whether you are on the "inside" or where you reside in the community.

The exercises then, are to help you, if: you are unable to talk about your feelings, if you are unable to forgive, if aggressive behavior (violence) is a problem for you. Other exercises are a Bible Study, and 'Testimony in Christ'. If God can change my life, and for example the life of book contributor, Tejuanis "Butch" Cassidy, who served 23 years in prisons, I know He can change your life. To those who struggle no matter what the reason, to write a letter, there is also an exercise to meet that need.

On the "inside" the workbook can be used by one person or several persons in a group, with a facilitator such as chaplain, community member, or church prison ministry representative. Within the community, the workbook may facilitate a course, by correspondence. Whichever you choose to meet your certain needs, the key to addictions recovery and inmate rehabilitation must be the word of God.

Some history:

A copy of my and our previous two books titled ***Connection to Freedom***, and ***Connection to Freedom Addictions Recovery Workbook*** was sent to a Chaplain in Texas, a Chaplain in California, and a copy went to a youth in Hawaii who was in jail. The Connection to Freedom book was a program of inner healing, as I interviewed alcoholics, drug addicts, inmates, and parolees, and of the street community. This, in most cases, brought healing to the interviewee.

The Connection to Freedom Addictions Recovery Workbook enabled me to hold a meeting for addicts, at the Central Baptist Church, and Mustard Seed Street Church. I donated 15 copies to the Chaplains at the Vancouver Island Regional Correctional Centre. I also donated a book to Ben and Germaine who ministered to the inmates at the Chuckwalla State Prison, in Blythe, California. You will find it interesting that 'youth at risk' are sometimes referred to in the personal stories.

I wish to thank Pastor Aneil of the Connection to Freedom Community Church, Duncan, BC, Canada, for his willingness to accept the workbook and overall program.

This workbook will be available on *Amazon.com* and *Amazon.ca*. (Keep checking back)

"I'll never forgive or forget!"

In my childhood, when I was eight or nine, I suffered debilitating asthma attacks. And being an introvert who was shy, didn't help me when it came to making school friends. The doctor had done every treatment that was possible, and always warned me about wearing a hat when it was raining, to avoid foggy days and to participate in breathing classes at the local hospital.

Because of my breathing challenges I was unable to play sports with some neighborhood boys who were kicking a football. Embarrassed and feeling unworthy, as hard as anyone, I tried to run the length of the field. I had even found a discarded pair of boots and had them on when mom called across the field: "He's not like you boys my son is sickly! You better send him home now!" I was feeling worthless amid the laughter from some of my mates, so I went home. In my bedroom although I was brokenhearted, I refused to shed any tears.

One particularly cold and foggy morning when my asthma was close to being debilitating, I was at school when our class was given a surprising uplift. Our teacher's personal interpretation of some verses from her copy of the Holy Bible surprised me. This was not part of the school itinerary it was something she did on her own each day before classes. Our teacher was a gentle-spirited woman who reminded me of my soft-spoken grandma who I loved dearly.

Imagining myself walking beside Bible characters, such as "Jesus" or "His disciples" to me was refuge from the storms of my asthma attacks and reality. In fact, learning about the Bible was the driving force that I looked forward to every morning. I was inspired to attend Sunday school classes to learn more. Whether I was wheezing or having a good day I enjoyed listening to the Bible stories.

My daydreams were shattered one morning when at school some money went missing. Because the so called "victim" sat in front of me all the students' eyes were on my area. My breathing became labored, and I felt my cheeks turn red with embarrassment. I wanted to climb under my desk, but I was too afraid to even move. My shyness because of asthma saw me as the laughingstock for some pupils.

I could not imagine any pain that was worse than being made to look like the class clown. But the grey haired, gentle spirited woman who was our teacher, pointed at me and in front of the class called me "thief!" My pain became worse, much worse. I had stolen nothing! But in that moment of sorrow, I felt deep resentment and walked away from God and any interest in her Bible, and I even quit Sunday school that until then I had attended every Sunday morning.

Our family's next move was to a coal mining village near Mansfield. Because of the polluted air, almost daily I found it difficult to breathe. But I wanted nothing to do with God, Jesus, the Bible. My schoolteacher, *I vowed to never forgive her*. And I was worried that if my dad heard about me being a thief, he would explode with anger, and I'd get a beating. When I was fifteen my dad had beat me so fiercely that I lost consciousness, and then he kicked me in the head, I was told by a neighbor who saw the madness. ***Never would I forgive him***. Dad died of cancer when I was sixteen. Often while yelling at me, he had forecast that I would, "be in jail by the time I was nineteen!"

My downward spiral took about a year: I was expelled from senior high school for bad behavior. I had conflicts with the Saanich Police about stealing a car and with the Victoria Police for stealing a radio. For discharging a firearm in the municipality of Saanich, a Juvenile Court judge made me pay a fine. The Royal Canadian Navy denied me entry because of my asthma history. Mom kicked me out of the house for my behavior that according to her was "incorrigible". So, at 17 years old I was homeless, and unemployed and drunk.

I slept a few nights in a borrowed sleeping bag at Mount Douglas Park (PKOLS) and then with a couple of friends I couch surfed and with a welfare cheque I paid for three days and nights at a hotel, and with shared bathroom and toilet facilities I rented a Richmond Avenue attic space for $25 a month.

With the rest of my money through a 30-year-old friend, I bought the liquor store's cheapest wine. But I made sure to save a few dollars, first for cigarettes and then a ferry ride to Vancouver. I had decided to get away from Victoria and travel to the Okanagan where I could live in a picker's cabin and work picking apples. I invited two pals, both roughly my age, to join me and they accepted.

We caught the ferry to Vancouver and to Abbotsford we took the bus. I had gone through half a pack of cigarettes since morning, so my first concern was to buy another pack. We talked it over and decided to save money by hitchhiking to the Okanagan. Unfortunately, we did not see the highway sign that thumbing rides was illegal. So after an hour when a police cruiser stopped we were surprised.

We must have displayed arrogance to the police because we were driven to Abbotsford's local jail. We spent roughly 24 hours in the lock-up. We were told by the jailor the cells "served as a drunk tank" on Friday nights and weekends. We played cards and drank coffee while we sat on the iron cots in cells. I showed phony identification to the police and got away with it but the three of us were interrogated about all kinds of crimes.

My two pals were allowed to phone their parents for the fare back to Victoria, but me being homeless, anyway, I had no one to phone. The policeman who was serving as our jailor with a warning about hitchhiking released me a short time after my friends.

I had no money, so I walked to the highway, and started hitchhiking again.

Kidnapped and abused

With my eyes trained on the highway for police cars, I was hoping that a ride would come quickly. With one hand grasping my blue tote bag and my other hand with my thumb out, I felt like I was hitching to "nowhere". My only companion was confusion with desperation that was growing. I could not forget how before my dad's death usually in anger, he always barked "You'll be in jail by the time you are 19!" He was wrong because I was 17, I assured myself as I climbed into the back seat of a car that had stopped for me.

Two more rides and an hour wait, and I was near Chilliwack or was it Mission, I wasn't sure. The first signs of nightfall were beginning to show, and my spirit was uplifted when a car driven with unfamiliar license plates waited for me on the side of the road. I ran with my blue canvas bag swinging from side to side. The driver was a big man with reddish hair in the form of a crew cut. He told me to climb in the back and to keep watch for police who might be following him. When he saw my furrowed brow questioning his reasoning he said, "I'm a United States lawman chasing a killer!" He made sure that I saw his shoulder holster and pistol, "a .38 caliber", he said.

"My purpose for keeping watch for police", he said was because of "jurisdiction disputes between Canada and the USA". When he showed me his badge and identification, a chill went through me! I could tell those were phony. When he asked me if I had ever fired a gun, thinking it could make me appear tougher, but without referring to my fine by Juvenile Court, boldly I replied, "Yes, I fired a rifle a couple of times!" He seemed unimpressed. And the violence and anger that radiated from him reminded me of my dad, and of the fear that used to grip me before every beating he gave me.

When the headlights of an oncoming vehicle revealed the man's eyes to me, I saw how lifeless they were, and I knew I had better get out of his car. But the nightmarish journey on the highway suddenly changed direction and he drove up a rocky road and came to a stop. He switched off the motor. I was frozen by fear and could do nothing! Through the car windows nothing human could be seen. He had told me this was his first trip to Canada but because of the way he drove that bumpy road with no concern for damage to his car, this showed me it was not his first time in British Columbia, never mind, Canada.

He told me more than asked me, to sit up front, so I could find him a certain country and western station on the radio. That was a dead giveaway that he was familiar with BC. How did he know about that local radio show? While in the front seat looking for the radio station I'd been asked to locate, I saw more than felt, a bright flash! I was unconscious! How long I was out cold I don't know but when I regained a semblance of awareness, I had no recollection. I had no idea of having been a passenger in a car or of the driver. I stood there trembling, and feeling like I had tumbled down concrete steps, somewhere. Nausea, pain, utter confusion was all I was aware of in that dark and bushy land.

I heard the faint rattling of an engine but then the noise subsided. I felt sick to my stomach and my clothes were covered in fresh mud. My hands were dirty, and I found it hard to stand up. I was utterly confused! I tried to think but failed to remember anything, believing only that I had fallen on concrete steps, banging my head.

The experience was horrifying but as the human mind will do in such horrific events for the sake of self-preservation all recollection of the tragic event was blocked as repressed memories. But, with a feeling of guilt I blamed myself desiring only to do self-harm and never questioning why.

I could see what looked like a tiny light. Carefully, one difficult step after another, I trod in the gravel and mud, toward the light that had become brighter. Then I was standing under a house porch light in the early dawn. I was face to face with two First Nations people: a grandmother and her grandson, I was to find out.

They questioned my state of sheer confusion, and the reason for my disheveled and dirty clothes. But when they each saw I had absolutely no recollection of even where I was, they stopped questioning me and gave me help. In fact, they saved my life that terrifying night. The elder and the youth, who was about my age, 17, gave me fresh clothing, meals, and a place to sleep. When I asked them where I was, they told me "Stave Lake, BC, Canada."

Unaware of the abuse I had suffered from my kidnapper, I returned to Victoria and visited my mom. She said, "The police were here to see me about you! Something to do with a stolen radio!" "I phoned your uncle in California, and I told him you were looking for work. He said if you moved down to California, he would help you get a job!" A feeling was pushing me to run away. I accepted mom's suggestion that I move to California, and she paid for the plane, and gave me enough money for a couple of weeks living with my uncle. She was convinced I would find work right away.

A month later as the plane left Vancouver, secretly I was nipping on a bottle of wine, in my travel case. Hours passed. The plane landed in the Mojave Desert where my uncle met me, and that night we got seriously drunk. He had moved to Southern California from Chicago, Illinois. A thumb nail sketch of my almost two years in California: I worked briefly in Apple Valley, I worked in Victorville, where I bought a car, Los Gatos, where I lost my car for driving drunk, and the Greater Mojave Desert town of Trona, where I worked, and was fired, and became homeless. I slept here and there but my friends turned away from me when I started drinking, "I was a wino at 18".

On July 4th, which I had celebrated already for six months, with alcohol, I walked away from my last drink of beer, and with less than ten cents in my pocket, I laid myself down on a windswept desert highway brightened only by the star sprinkled desert sky. I had no fear, no regrets, and one month shy of my 19th birthday, I made peace with my decision to end my life. I heard a car speeding on its way, to Bakersfield, and I fell fast asleep. A car ran over me, and left me bloody, broken, and near death, on the highway, two miles west of Inyokern, the newspaper, 'The Bakersfield Californian' had published.

Two sailors from the base at China Lake, discovered me lying on the windswept desert highway. They contacted the California Highway Patrol and the Ridgecrest Community Hospital who sent an ambulance. After two further hospitalizations, Kern County General and in Victoria, BC, the Royal Jubilee, I became addicted to the pain killer morphine. At twenty-three or so, I became addicted to a drug with similar chemical properties to morphine, but more potent, heroin!! To support my addiction, which was very costly, my girlfriend was a junkie too, I became involved with crime, and criminals such as I had also become.

Psych Ward and Jail

I had staggered into the Victoria police station with a broken wine bottle in my hand. I saw the first uniform and intended to slash the police officer. A deep voice called "Steve!" and I went out like a light. "Suicide by cop" was my deranged and drunken plan. I found myself in the psych ward at Eric Martin a psychiatric hospital. Only I did not know it because I thought I was visiting somebody there. Adults dressed in blue coloured pajamas were shuffling along in paper slippers, doped up like zombies. An old man was trying to choke himself, while at the same time, a young woman was yelling at the top of her lungs. There was no doubt this was a hospital for the mentally ill men and women of different ages. "But what am I doing here? I must be visiting someone. Yes, I am just waiting for them to show up. I have been waiting a long time! Wonder what is taking so long?" These were the thoughts that dripped through my mind.

Nervously I glanced down at a man reading a newspaper, he looked as though he had shoved a wet finger into a live electric socket. His hair stood on end and his expression was permanent shock! In the kitchen, there was big noise. The clanging sounds of pots and clattering of dishes reached my ears. I became vaguely aware that the people were having supper, or lunch or it was breakfast. I began to sense fear within me as I realized that I was holding a tray of food. Worse than this, I was also wearing blue pajamas and paper slippers. Shuffling along like a zombie, day after day in a chemical comfort zone of anti-depressants, and a codeine-based pain killer for my headaches, I could not grasp any part of human existence.

But the worst moments at the hospital were my middle of the night 'cold sweats.' With perspiration dripping from every poor I tried to write about my feelings. But I had no writing paper in that moment of desperation. So I used the inside liner of a garbage can, and when that didn't work, I scribbled on my pillow furiously. The next morning my scribblings would be shown to a psychiatrist, by a nurse who had taped my writings to the Nurses Station wall. That's how I communicated my feelings with the doctors. Never did I talk about my kidnapping and abuse.

I had taken an extensive written Psych Test, and days later the Analyst told me that according to my answers I was suited for "public speaking" and "religion". How ridiculous! Public speaking at school had frightened me and religion I ignored as if it was a plague. Boy, did she ever make a mistake!

During my hospitalization I had lost my workers compensation board case. I was not mentally able to respond to their requests by letter. And when a psychologist was trying to help me to "get in touch with my feelings," I suffered a massive epileptic seizure in front of my fellow patients. According to a psychologist, I was "not ready to deal with my feelings."

After about three months that included once or twice in a padded cell, I left the hospital. I had only my welfare cheque to look forward to, no address, and with one prescription being a codeine-based headache medication, and bottles for depression, and insomnia. My youngest brother helped me with a place to stay, but I kept popping pills, getting blitzed out of my head, and have no memory of that time and place, other than my psychiatrist, when I went to see him, offered me little comfort, and wouldn't give me any pills. A couple of years later I stood before a provincial court judge while my defense lawyer, said: "Your Honour, Mr. Bradley is unfit to be in the community, to await his hearing. He should stay at Wilkinson Road Jail!" Before that a nurse at the Victoria police station asked if I felt suicidal because I was coming off opioids. I lied saying, "No!"

Out at the jail I was in a dingy cell at the end of the tier. I was looking for something to hang myself with. But an inmate's voice distracted me: "Hey buddy, do you want a sandwich and a cup of coffee?" This was certainly not my first time in this jail but never was there such a "warm welcoming committee" as that inmate. His kind words shocked me! And that may have saved my life. I thought about my crime. I was so sick; I had picked up a boulder and heaved it through a plate glass front door of a drug store. I climbed through the broken glass and when four Victoria police officers caught me, I was sitting on the floor furiously rummaging through a pile of prescriptions looking for narcotics.

I stood before the judge wearing an old coat, my hair was a mess and I had blood stains on my light blue jeans. I cannot explain it, my defense lawyer did me a favour when he told the judge to send me to Wilkinson

Road Jail to await my hearing. I received a six-month jail sentence and a year probation. Did the judge see the sheer desperation in my life, and took pity on me? I was drug- sick and it was obvious to me mental illness was mine as well.

Or was it that God had chosen me for "public speaking" about "religious matters" as the Eric Martin Analyst had proclaimed? Still, I could never talk about my feelings.

The "Feelings Chart," which is next, is a way for you to "connect" with your feelings.

"My Feelings" Exercise

Writing about your feelings can be an important part of self-rehabilitation. You can choose whether to record your feelings by the day or by the month or both. Use the words from this list.

Feelings Word List

Aggressive, Agonized, Anxious, Apologetic, Arrogant, Bashful, Blissful, Bored, Cautious, Cold, Concentrating, Confident, Curious, Degraded, Determined, Disappointed, Tearful, Disapproving, Disbelieving, Disgusted, Distasteful, Ecstatic, Enraged, Envious, Exasperated, Exhausted, Enthusiastic, Frightened, Frustrated, Grief, Guilty, Happy, Horrified, Hopeful, Horrendous, Hurt, Hysterical, Indifferent, Idiotic, Innocent, Interested, Jealous, Joyful, Lonely, Meditative, Mischievous, Miserable, Negative, Obstinate, Optimistic, Pained, Paranoid, Perplexed, Proud, Puzzled, Regretful, Relieved, Sad, Satisfied, Shocked, Sheepish, Smug, Surly, Surprised, Suspicious, Sympathetic, Suicidal, Thoughtful, Undecided, Withdrawn, Afraid, Exasperated, Motivated, Unforgiveness, Forgiveness, Grateful, Thankful, Appreciated, Uplifting, Belief, Lovingly, Friendly, Courage, Homesickness.

My Chart

(Day 1) "I'm feeling_____ today."

(Month 1) "I'm feeling_____today."

(Day 2) "I'm feeling_____today."

(Month 2) "I'm feeling_____today."

(Day 3) "I'm feeling_____today."

(Month 3) "I'm feeling_____today."

(Day 4) "I'm feeling_____today."

(Month 4) "I'm feeling_____today."

(Day 5) "I'm feeling_____today."

(Month 5) "I'm feeling_____today."

(Day 6) "I'm feeling_____today."

(Month 6) "I'm feeling_____today."

(Day 7) "I'm feeling_____today."

(Month 7) "I'm feeling_____today."

Be of good courage, and He shall strengthen your
heart, all you who hope in the Lord.
Psalm 31:24

My Addiction to Alcohol

I was still on Probation from Victoria and had transferred to an Edmonton Probation Officer who suggested I look for work "up north". I found work as a miner in Thompson, Manitoba. At least it would keep me from committing another burglary and going to jail.

After being employed at the mine for a couple of months, due to a careless accident below ground, I was abruptly let go by management. But I was happy to leave the blinding snow squalls and bitterly cold temperatures that had accompanied me.

During one of my binges, I decided to go to The Pas, a couple of hundred miles away. I was joined by two other ex-miners who had also had their fill of the North Country. One of my travelling companions was Billy, an ex-boxer from Edmonton, and the other was Ron, from Saskatchewan whose nose I had broken two weeks earlier in a fight. Nobody carried a grudge because that's just the way it was in those northern mining communities.

Arriving at The Pas Railroad Station, blind drunk, I walked off with someone else's suitcase. Totally unaware of my mistake, and getting more intoxicated, I sat with Billy and Ron at a noisy coffee shop. My head was nodding back and forth to rock music from an old jukebox when suddenly the three of us were looking at the faces of RCMP officers who had come looking for us and the "stolen" suitcase.

The Mounties transported us to their Station and charged us with theft over 50 dollars. But I suspected there was more to this than simple theft.

After an hour or more of interrogation by the Mounties, Billy, Ron, and I were sent to The Pas Provincial Jail. We were kept in the dormitory, which had double bunk beds and a card table. After a meal of cold spaghetti and warm tea and dressed in khaki colored jail issue I lay on my bunk, listening to the lonesome sound of a howling wind.

Wolf, an inmate in the lower bunk, said he was 49 years old, but he looked 89. The consequences of hard living, alcoholism and crime were written across his face in deep wrinkles. He spoke with me a great deal about his addiction, and I questioned my own drinking habits. Meanwhile, chaotic thoughts of my California experiences filled my mind and morphine injections. In my recollections, I marveled at how the painkiller had eased my pain so well and removed my emotional torment.

At nightfall when the jail was filled with the sounds of heavy snoring, coughing and other noises, I felt what I believed was an inner force influencing me. I had no definition in my mind or any clear vision but deep within me was an indescribable longing for help from some power beyond my understanding. Oh, it wasn't that a prison chaplain could have explained this to me because I would not have listened. No this was a private, and I do mean private, connection. But to what I did not know.

As I listened to the wind roar and pellets of ice batter the barred windows, deep in my heart I felt sorrow. However, with the next gust of wind, this feeling was gone. Days later, in court standing before a crowd of parka-clad onlookers, I felt ashamed for standing up and firing my lawyer. Despite the tough guy image that I extended to the world; I had caught sight of the other side of me. However, I could not allow this vulnerable part of me to show.

Two weeks later the real reason that the RCMP had arrested us was revealed. It had nothing to do with theft of over 50 dollars but was more to make an example of our type of person. The judge, a small man, seated at a majestic judicial bench, related how the citizens of The Pas were tired of miners coming down from Thompson and causing mischief with their drinking. He warned: "Next time we will make an example of you, so stay out of The Pas!"

Not for another twenty years would I admit to being an alcoholic.

My Addiction to Morphine

At the Ridgecrest Community Hospital, I overheard a conversation, by doctors, "There's no good putting a splint on his leg, he's not going to last the night." Those words made me very angry, and I thought to myself, "what right do they have to say I won't last the night? They don't know how tough I am! Somebody should tell them I'm going to fight hard to stay alive!" Midnight ice baths to lower my temperature, my broken pelvis, my fractured right ankle, and injuries that would require a colostomy, made my pain so excruciating that I almost cried in agony! No matter how hard I tried, I could not audibly express my needs, I had totally lost my voice! The only brightness for me was the twice daily morphine injections which as the addict mind thinks, seemed to make it all worthwhile.

After weeks, I was well enough to be transferred to Kern County General Hospital, where I continued to receive injections of morphine as pain treatment. Doctors decided I should be returned to Victoria, due to difficulties with my medical coverage, and their concern about a possible medical malpractice suit. So, by Air Ambulance which was a nightmare of nausea, thanks to my mom's friend, I was flown home. When the plane landed in Victoria, a Saanich Police car escorted an ambulance, that took me to the Royal Jubilee Hospital where strapped to a circular bed, I received morphine injections for my pain.

I received visitors to include a former girlfriend, my two cousins, and old friends. Mom, and my youngest brother, Ian, were regular visitors, but nothing made me feel as happy, relaxed, and confident, as after my regular injection of morphine. One morning my first thoughts were of a needle with morphine, so automatically, I pressed the alarm to the Nurses' Station, pleading, in my well-rehearsed sickly voice, "I've got a lot of pain, I need something for pain!" The Head Nurse injected me with the joy I'd been waiting for, the confidence, and the intelligence, morphine! She then said, "We're going to be taking you off morphine or else you'll become addicted to it, and when you leave hospital, you'll be looking for it on the streets!" Mentally, I flew into a blind rage! "What right does she have to take me off morphine, it is my right!"

Two orderlies lifted me from my circular bed, and I was placed in a regular bed, and wheeled into the Isolation ward. "Mild pain killers", were my only option according to a nurse, answering my plea for morphine. My nights were haunted by ghastly looking creatures, that were mocking me! I closed my eyes tightly trying to rid myself of the skeletal demons that were swimming in my hot and cold sweats, and I screamed for them to leave me alone! One day, one night, one day, one night, as I began to look better physically, according to a nurse, I was totally aware that, there was no doubt whatever, I was addicted to morphine, and I would be looking for it on the street.

When I was released from the hospital but knew I had to return for more surgery, I was taken to my mother's house by ambulance. There, I was assisted with a Red Cross hospital bed, and daily visits by a nurse. Mom worked as a nurse at a Senior's hospital, afternoon shift, mainly. I had the house to myself on many occasions, walked on crutches and awaited my return to the hospital for surgery related to my colostomy. **But I was looking forward to more morphine injections.**

My Addiction to Heroin

It was 1969 when I first started using and dealing heroin. But several years later after being busted for a burglary charge, I was locked up in cells at the Victoria Police Station, being questioned by a detective. He asked me about everything from a burglary to a robbery of a Credit Union.

As my body yearned for the magic-powder called heroin, I trembled so badly that I was unable to fasten my coat. I almost admitted to the robbery because I was too sick to argue. Then, days later at Wilkinson Road Jail, I shuffled along the tier with a blanket wrapped around my shoulders.

Then a junkie acquaintance came to my cell. I asked for his long underwear or his coat as he was not sick. But he responded with some dribble like, "I can't give you my jacket or underwear because the guards will charge me with helping you escape!" Funny how tough this guy acted on the outside but behind bars he was a blithering idiot. A couple of years later some crazed dealer who he had ripped off in Vancouver would put a bullet in him.

The guy in the next cell, one of my partners, was a Satanist and close friend, and he was seeing an orange cat in his hallucinations. Red, who had come with me when I shot a rifle at a dealer, slashed his wrists, and was carried out of his cell on a stretcher, by two guards. He yelled out to me, "I did it for you, Steve!"

A guard came to the gate when we threatened to smash up our cells if we didn't get proper medical help for our withdrawals. There were about 8 or so deathly sick junkies on my tier. I yelled at one of the guards and threatened to smash up my cell, but he just laughed, hollering back at me: "Go ahead, smash up your cell, Bradley; that's what we're here for!" There was complete chaos!

The media was contacted by an unknown inmate and later that night we learned the jail was going to be issuing methadone tablets. But it would take a lot more than we were to receive from the doctor to get straight.

We "junkies" decided to play poker for our methadone tablets. The winner would be feeling a lot better while the losers would suffer. This card game was like hell on earth. Our tier was designated by the jail guards as the "junkies' tier".

This time in my life was my worst nightmare: "the walk of the living dead."

The guy who slashed his wrists sold one cap of my heroin to an undercover cop and it cost him 6 years in the Matsqui Institution.

"I'm in VIRCC again!"

My withdrawal from alcohol, heroin and other opioids caused a lot worse pain than I had experienced before when entering jail. I stayed in my cell because I was too sick to associate with any other human beings. Eventually, however, I was well enough to socialize, that is, to find myself a drug "connection." I injected heroin that was shared with me by an inmate in our unit. His criminal charge was related to heroin transportation. It turned out that he and an ex-girlfriend of mine had worked together in the drug business. Before breakfast, I picked up my medication at the dispensary, Phenobarbital, and Dilantin. I've had epilepsy for fifteen years. At meals, I sometimes ate with an inmate who was charged with murder, another with manslaughter and a third who was a drug dealer. Getting sentenced for the attempted robbery of a drug store was my "claim to fame," but eighteen months I felt was a gift from above.

In the summer heat, my cell sometimes felt like the inside of an oven. The record-breaking temperatures we experienced didn't help my concentration as I read myself to sleep. I heard a knocking on my cell door. I looked up and peering at me through the small glass window was Harvey, a biker type, from two cells down. I asked him to come in and climbed off my bunk. Harvey and I were from the "old school" where you didn't enter another inmate's cell without first being invited. Harvey, who was seven years older than me (I was forty-one), invited me down to his cell to look at a new biker magazine he had received in the mail. Because I was bored stiff, I accepted his invitation.

We smoked our cigarettes and drank the joint's coffee while sharing our failures and successes in recovery from our addictions. Where my "poisons" of choice were alcohol, heroin and opioid pills, Harvey's were booze and marijuana. I don't know what started us talking about recovery because I thought he had wanted to share some drugs with me. He didn't. Maybe we were just sick and tired of coming to jail. Harvey suggested, "Why don't we start a program of our own, Steve? You know real recovery must come from us!" At 10:30 a.m., because we ignored the buzzer, the

18

unit officer called out, "Lock up!" and, reluctantly, I returned to my cell until lunchtime when our doors would again be opened.

I sat there on the edge of my bunk staring through the barred window at the wire fence and the high-powered surveillance camera. In the distance was a scene that reminded me of our family home near Mount Douglas. I was reminded of how when I was fifteen, my dad punched me in the face and (as I was to learn) knocked me out. While I was unconscious, he booted me in the head. This behavior I had known since I was eight years old. My mom told me that dad couldn't help it because he had "a violence sickness," and she always wrote notes to my teachers whenever I had a black eye, fat lip, or severe scratches. But when I was sixteen, at thirty-nine, my dad died of cancer. (An inmate yelling at another guy took me from my self-pity and back into 1987 and my time living in Unit D. There in my cell I thought about Harvey's suggestion that we inmates should "start our own program.")

But what could we do for ourselves in these near-maximum-security conditions? We couldn't make a single move from our living area without filling out a request form and receiving permission from officers, including courtyard escorts and permission from the deputy director. Special OKs would be given only after these requests had filtered through to the officer in charge of our living unit. No, I couldn't see any way to start a program of our own.

It was the second week of August and according to the unit information board, the biggest thing that was happening at VIRCC was a recovering addict from the community who would be speaking in a three-session seminar on alcohol and drug abuse. The dates: August 27, 28, and 29. With my addict mind working overtime, I decided to join Harvey and about twenty other inmates for the three-session lecture. But my purpose in going was just to see if I could con cigarettes out of the speaker and if he would take a kite (illegal note) out to a girlfriend. I'd try to get some drugs anyway I could. I was craving the euphoric rush that heroin and other opioids gave me.

The first two sessions revealed nothing new to me other than the speaker was not willing to break the rules to take a letter to my girlfriend. It had been written in code asking her to book a visit and bring me some heroin. My mind was not on the seminar talk or the recovery videos and, as far as cigarettes were concerned, the guy apparently didn't smoke cigarettes. Well, at least I had escaped the monotonous jail routine for an hour or more! But there was a deeper, darker truth. Before Harvey knocked on my cell door, I had suffered a horrendous cold-turkey withdrawal from alcohol, heroin, and opioids. In fact, I had nothing left. I had no will to live, only the motivation to end my life. Nonetheless, as I had throughout my life, I kept my feelings hidden behind a phony smile and too many jokes.

I dragged myself to the third session of the seminar. The speaker mentioned his membership in the twelve-step programs, AA, and NA, and described himself as "a recovering alcoholic and drug addict." He also explained his understanding of these programs, describing them as "spiritual, not religious." Suddenly an inmate called out, "I don't need those programs! What if I've got Jesus?" His tone was mocking. Some others, thinking it funny, joined the mouthy inmate. The speaker who had come to the jail to help us became annoyed. He spoke clearly: "I don't care if believing in Jesus is your thing! Whatever gets you clean and sober is what you need!" I didn't understand at that time the moving of my spirit or the hope that had come to me when the name "Jesus" was mentioned. Maybe it was just my imagination, but I felt stronger when I left the seminar that August evening.

But in my cell, as night closed over me and the lights shone under my cell door, I slipped further into suicidal desperation. I would use a bed sheet to hang myself, I thought in sheer hopelessness. With a pencil pushed against a quickly torn piece of paper, I began to write why I had killed myself, and that my mother shouldn't blame herself. Strangely, I felt pity for the corrections officer who in the morning would find my dead body. With my life hanging in the balance, the name of "Jesus," which was made fun of by the inmate in the seminar, flashed through my mind. I remembered how the speaker had reflected on the terms "self-will, willpower, ego, higher power, and God as individually understood" as in the twelve-step program. Divine intervention was something I had heard about way back in my past. But too many miles and not enough smiles had fogged up my recollection.

That night seemed like a terrible LSD trip as I watched the demons that had haunted me in my alcohol, heroin and opioid withdrawals mock me again! I had no strength to go on living. I knew that heroin and other opioids would never let go of me and that my alcoholism was also with me for life. Cigarettes too would not leave me. I plunged into the abyss of my sorrow. Although I could accept that I was only a harmless drunk and occasional pill popper, my addictions were rapidly turning me into a killer. I inspected my tattoos.

One was on my shoulder; it represented the remnants of a four-year relationship and defined my limit to self-sabotage with all my relationships. On my left forearm were two snakes in the form of a misshapen heart to remind me of my dabbling in Satanism in 1976. These designs had been made with a crude instrument, a toothbrush with three sewing needles melted into the end and dipped in India ink. I saw the lousy gang tattoo of a Butterfly on my left hand, that I received twenty years ago at Wilkinson Road Jail. Did these images represent who I really was? My right forearm had the best part of my story but the saddest. It was my dad's and my story and our family's story after his death. When I received this last tattoo from Red, seventeen years ago, I was as sick as a dog coming down from heroin in this very same jail.

That bleak August 29th night in 1987, tossing between life and death, I called out for help. "God, if you're real, I need your help! I've destroyed my life, and I've done it by myself!" A small still voice but with the power of a cascading waterfall, spoke to my spirit three words that totally changed my life: "Help these men!" Unaware of the reverence of these words, they were God's call on my life. But, amazed by the experience, responding to the Lord, I said in my spirit, "Me, how could I help anybody, Lord? Besides, I'm a drug addict myself. Aren't I?" I believe God answered me through His vision for my life, as follows:

I closed my eyes to sleep after thumbing through a bible that I had brought from the chapel. With spiritually reborn eyes, I was taken into the darkness of the jail's courtyard at night. My attention was drawn to a "light" that seemed to be miles above me. The sight and sound of a rapidly descending helicopter, carrying the "light," filled the courtyard. Suddenly, I saw the "light" brighten all areas of the jail. The helicopter had landed. Hearing the morning clatter and the sound of voices, I woke up with a jolt! Immediately I understood the meaning of my dream. It was God's will for me to spread His light, "the message of Jesus Christ in my life," throughout all areas of VIRCC. I knew without a doubt that Jesus Christ had forgiven me and saved me! (God's vision for my life.)

With my spirit transformed from suicidal desperation to a feeling of overwhelming joy, I stood on my cell floor transfixed, unable to recognize myself! I had never felt such lightness in my feet! The burdens I had placed on myself year after year, with my addictions and related criminality seemed to have disappeared! My purpose, to serve Jesus Christ through His vision for my life, had already begun. The change in me was so dramatic that as strange as it might seem, I knew that through the Lord, I would spend the rest of my life helping others. Immediately, I felt the spirits of anger and violence from inmates who wanted to shut me down. But the lightness, and yet power, of the Holy Spirit strengthened me. Anytime I spoke the name of Jesus, which was all day long, every day, spirits contrary to Him, from morning to night, pushed against me.

The Birth of Connection to Freedom

I began to share Christ's love by making coffee in the mornings and serving my fellow inmates. I asked them how they felt about coming to a meeting in my cell. Two or three responded and appealed to me for help with various needs. I was now lending an ear to quite a few inmates. As I prayed and asked the Lord's guidance, He revealed that a Christ-centered meeting was His will for inmates with addictions.

An F Unit inmate, who wanted to talk with me about his recovery, had been assaulted by another prisoner and he had suffered a broken nose. But, with permission from our unit officer who contacted the other officer, I went to see the wounded inmate. I say "wounded" because I knew that his pride had been wounded, even crushed. When I was inside Unit F, the air was thick with spirits of violence, anger, and hatred, that blew against me like a hot wind.

The inmate whose nose was broken wanted to hide in his cell, but I spoke to the inmate group, who seemed to be a threat to him, loudly and confidently. To sneers and angry looks, I confessed my hope in Jesus Christ. Some inmates who knew me from the outside thought I was running a scam. A day or two later an inmate who called himself a "Christian," which I knew was a lie, asked me to write a letter of support for his court hearing.

"I didn't realize how much power you had in this jail, and I hope you use it for good things only!" said our unit officer.

A week later, some inmates encircled me in the courtyard and tried to intimidate me, saying, "Check yourself into protective custody or you're going to get hurt! Stop preaching about Jesus and upsetting the way things are supposed to be in jail!"

It didn't take a genius to become aware that inmates who had shared with me their faith in God seemed to be hiding when they thought I was going to get a beating or be killed. I was walking into places of spiritual darkness and evil and I knew it. But I was never without the power of the Holy Spirit to caution and protect me. In my cell, there were times when I felt alone and fearful, but I knew that God inhabited the praises of His people, so, my praise to Him was my weapon. This certain day after I gave a bible to an inmate in the courtyard, he became angry and threw it as far as he could. His rage, it turned out, was because he couldn't read. Later he told me his story, but he refused to accept Christ. In my cell at night, I prayed harder for him.

I was attending Friday evening bible group, presented by the prison ministry of Trinity Christian Centre, and Sunday gospel and music meetings of the Church of The Way, delivered by Don and Marg Baker. Going to and from the chapel often earned me a dirty look, or a demeaning remark, from inmates and one or two correctional officers. Some inmates in my unit, who I had been helping through the Lord, asked me to bring them each a bible from the chapel. Going back to my cell after the service, I was searched by an officer, who asked, "What have you got hidden in those bibles, Bradley?" I reacted with anger. His question stung my ego, and I was caught off balance. "I've got guns and drugs, what do you think!" But that night before lock-up I handed out eight bibles. One inmate who was known as extremely violent, telephoned his mother to say, "Hey, mom, we've got a family bible now!"

Following lunch a few days later an inmate who was worried about losing his drug mule to my "Christian ways" pleaded with me, saying, "Steve, you know what it's like to go cold turkey in this joint! I need my guy because he's got my drugs. Don't turn him sober. Promise me, OK? Look, I don't know if you're conning the whole jail or what!" I stared into his eyes which seemed to lack any life. He continued: "I don't care if the other inmates follow you like the Pied Piper, just leave my guy alone. He's just been moved to your unit!" After I invited him to receive Jesus Christ, the inmate angrily stormed away as if he thought I was a madman. On the street five years earlier, he and I were scoring heroin from the same dealer. Another guy was there who'd had his finger chopped off for not paying a drug debt.

That afternoon while many inmates went to the gym and the exercise yard and weight pit, I stayed in my cell and prayed. Just as I had heard the words, "Help these men," in my spirit, once again I heard not with my ears but deep inside of me, "Give the fellowship a name." It was still a small voice, but it seemed to have the power of an enormous cascading waterfall.

On September 1st, from morning until night I was moved, not by personal desire but by the Holy Spirit, to find a name for the group of inmates who were seeking my help. The Lord, I felt, must have seen us prisoners as a fellowship because all I talked about was Jesus Christ and how He had saved me and was keeping me from drugs. Prayerfully, I looked for and found a cardboard canteen box about the size of a shoebox. I wrote a label: "Suggestions for our name." Then I made a slit on the top of the box for ideas to be submitted. Alternating the suggestion box between my Unit D and the adjoining Unit C, with each officer's permission, I also wrote and deposited my own idea, which was "Escape to Reality."

As inmates submitted their written names, I watched, feeling proud of my accomplishment. That night I remembered how while I was out on bail, almost a year earlier, I was ordered by the judge to attend some Narcotics Anonymous meetings for my heroin and opioid problems. So, to collect support letters for me for court, I had complied with my bail officer's request.

My first meeting was in the evening at an elementary school. As the NA group rambled on, I was invited to tell my story. Feeling embarrassed among the strangers I felt my voice quiver as I spoke: "I had gone to pick up some heroin in New Westminster with some other guys who badly needed the 'junk' as well. At the 'buy,' we were robbed by a tall greasy-haired 'junkie' who was holding a revolver and a short man with a sawn-off shotgun who was barking orders! 'Put your hands up and give us your money or we'll shoot you!' There were four or five of us, trembling with cold turkey shakes. There was more to come that day. After I used a rifle to rob a dealer for money to buy heroin, there was such a chaotic scene when I stuck the barrel of the rifle into the guy's gut. He was having a seizure! I hid the rifle behind a heat register and ran for my life. But that afternoon I returned to retrieve the rifle that I had hidden before the police arrived.

The chairperson of the Narcotics Anonymous group blew me away when he said, "We're not here to brag about our shortcomings, we are here to support the newcomer. But, thanks, Steve, for sharing your story." My ego was severely bruised. September 2nd, almost bubbling over with self-adoration, I emptied the suggestion box on a card table. There were sixteen suggestions. The same number of inmates that constituted a unit had contributed ideas for names. But we couldn't decide which name was best. Just then an inmate, a French-Canadian weightlifter, returning from the exercise yard, called out, "Hey, I see how you guys are trying to find a name. You're trying to get away from drugs, so you need a different connection from the drug connections you've got in jail here. You're trying to get free from drugs and booze, right? So why not call yourselves 'Connection to Freedom'?" The inmates who had been standing around the table trying to choose the best name looked at each other. We all knew that the best name had now been chosen by God, whether we believed in Him or not. It was a moment that could not be denied. I felt ashamed of my prideful feelings of losing control. But when the Lord gave us this name, I understood how He was in control, the leader of the fellowship, not me! Clearly, I understood that a meeting had to be held. On the evening of September 7th, twelve inmates attended the meeting at which I was the facilitator.

I had never led any kind of group in my life and had only spoken at a court-ordered NA meeting. I was afraid of public speaking and had always avoided it in school. But the Lord had inspired me to hustle all day long, collecting chairs from the cells and placing a blanket over a ping pong table in the C Unit laundry/recreation area. I had also put a written request in for coffee many days earlier, but still, it did not arrive. However, we managed to find some.

The meeting itself was chaotic with each man for himself. I tried to remember what I had seen at twelve-step meetings over the years. But these men in this meeting were not only drug addicts and/or alcoholics but violent drug pushers and thieves and, like me, drugstore robbers and as society saw some, much worse. When crosstalk at our founding "inmates with addictions" meeting became too disruptive and slipped out of my control, I threatened violence if they didn't settle down. "Listen," I said, "I might not be that big but if you keep butting in like that I'll climb over this table and give you a shot in the head." I was dumbfounded by my words and my behaviour when I slammed my fist hard on the table! When the French-Canadian weightlifter began to smile at me, I said: "This means you too!" Nevertheless, we voted unanimously to accept the name he had submitted, "Connection to Freedom." Sadly, just three days after one of our group members was released, he died from taking a prescription of sleeping pills with opioids.

From one end of the jail to the other, the name "Connection to Freedom" was being talked about. No corrections officers at VIRCC had ever seen or heard of anything like inmates building their own recovery program, such as Connection to Freedom. After we held several Connection to Freedom meetings, the prison's director of programs and services came to see me, saying he and his staff were concerned about this inmate movement. They didn't trust the men from other units, who had been putting in requests to attend. My angry response was: "If all inmates are not given the same opportunity to come to the meetings, I will end the group."

Although I believed it was the end of the Connection to Freedom meetings, I prayed to learn God's will. The answer to my prayer was a program in the form of a book. The regular members and other inmates from any area of the jail were now invited to write their stories and poems to place in a book to be called, what else, "Connection to Freedom." This book project saw twenty inmates come together. Instead of listening to their stories in my cell as at the beginning of the group, I would now read their personal accounts, and, in some cases, I sat with them and wrote as they told me about their lives.

It was suggested by my French-Canadian friend who gave us the name "Connection to Freedom" that I think about writing for parole, so I could get out and establish the meetings and the book program on the outside. Within a few weeks, I was notified that my application had been received by the parole coordinator. Janet, a volunteer from the community, typed our stories. My personal story included mention of the Apostle Paul. When Janet finished, she promised to bring our group-book back to the jail. Little did I know then, but she and I would spend a year in the outside community making a much bigger version of the book with "street stories."

An inmate asked me to write a letter to support him in court. My reply was, "No!" I knew no judge would put any stock in a letter from an inmate such as me. The guy who had requested the letter gave a final comment before leaving my cell in a huff. "There's too much God in that Connection to Freedom book!" Little did I know I would run into this inmate one night when I was working on the street.

A couple of weeks later, an inmate on the tier above me went crazy! He was yelling and screaming in anger! Not even the correctional officer in charge of our unit wanted to confront him. The pressure of the inmate's murder charge was getting to him. As I prayed silently to myself, the Holy Spirit quickened me to help the man.

After receiving the unit officer's permission, I invited the extremely angry inmate into my cell. He saw how unimpressed I was by his threats, when I said, "I've done heroin for eighteen years and been a dealer, and I've known more pain than you can imagine!" I asked him if I might pray for his needs. That's when I became involved in helping him. I read his trial transcripts and prayed for God's will, daily. Never did I sense the Lord wanted me to stop helping the troubled man. Over the unit telephone, I met his girlfriend who thanked me, and I shared my faith with her. I was laser focused as I continued to pray and work with the once "crazed" inmate. I marveled at the Lord's work and how even the toughest prisoners, of which he was one, had in some ways softened in spirit towards me.

The day of his trial I prayed for the inmate whose girlfriend I had spoken with over the unit telephone. His lawyer I would learn he "did not know where the words came from" in his defense. "Not guilty!" was the result and as far as I understood, God had intervened. That night of his acquittal I was talking with my girlfriend on the unit telephone. She said, "There's somebody here who wants to say hello to you. As I listened, I heard what I know was from the Lord: "Hey, Steve, you and Connection to Freedom helped me with your prayers, I believe!" His girlfriend echoed his thanks that I credited to Jesus Christ.

I began to think of myself as a counsellor while collecting the inmates' stories and using my cell as a counselling room. But while my ego was shining brightly the deputy director (deputy warden) came to our unit for cell inspection. When he saw a poster on my cell door "Connection to Freedom Counselling," angrily he had the unit officers tear my cell apart. I was yanked from my self-important comfort zone when the deputy said, "Who does he think he is?" It just so happened that within a day of my cell inspection, I was transferred from my living unit (D) to the kitchen unit (K) where I met Ted. He was an inmate who was very familiar through his own addiction and recovery with slips, failures, and successes, and he knew the meaning of "one day at a time," which I couldn't grasp. Before the night lock-up, I asked Ted, my fellow kitchen worker, if I could see him for a few minutes. He was receptive and invited me to sit and talk.

Nervously, feeling ashamed, I said, "I don't know what you're going to think of me, but what I've got to get off my chest is heavy. I believe it's disgusting. At least it feels that way to me!" Without showing much concern, Ted said, "It's going to be lock-up soon, Steve, so you better tell me what's on your mind or forget it until tomorrow!" There in that kitchen unit, **I had no idea that my kidnapping and abuse at seventeen near Stave Lake, BC, was the driving force that drove me to attempt suicide in California when I was one month short of my nineteenth birthday. I believed my pain was related to being bullied by racists.** So, I told Ted the only truth I knew:

"When I lived in the desert in California as a kid, racists, threatening me, drove me to try to kill myself. I lay on my back at night, July 4th, and I wanted a car to run over me and kill me. This was around the time of the Watts County riots. But, anyways, I was run over by a car that was speeding on its way to Bakersfield, and the driver didn't see me in the dark. I've never told anybody before that I tried to kill myself. I always said I was the victim of a hit-and-run accident. Nobody knows, man, only you. And that's how I got to be a heroin addict—from hospital morphine. Three years after that I got epileptic seizures."

Ted, unmoved by my nervous mumblings and my story, looked at me and said, "So what? Everybody's got their own story and it always seems to them to be the worst in the world. Steve, your story is typical of lots of addicts. You're not the only one!" In taking the time to listen to me, Ted did more for me than he could ever know. But there was something else I needed to get off my chest, to confess, I guess you'd call it. The Holy Spirit was leading me to unburden myself. The following, which I didn't unload to Ted, I was giving up to the Lord, not trying to keep it a secret from Him.

I was involved with Satanists, tore pages from a holy bible, and when it came to setting myself on fire in allegiance to Satan, I heard a small voice say, "You don't have to do this!" Then I saw the back of a hooded figure. As he turned, I was shocked to see that it was me! I found myself strapped to a bed at Saint Paul's Hospital. How can I doubt that God's hand even back then was on my life? I confessed further to the Lord: I accepted a contract to kill a guy who was thieving from his own kind. Four hundred dollars wasn't much for a human life. But I didn't see it that way in my cold-turkey shakes. I fired a rifle at the dealer who was robbing weaker dealers. I missed my aim but my two co-conspirators, both as sick as me, needing heroin, had forgotten to bring more cartridges. How can I believe anything, other than God, had his hand on my life? I decided not to tell these areas of my life to Ted. Besides, was I not confessing these sinful experiences to the Lord, not trying to deny them?

At the chapel, seventeen inmates attended my testimony and for the second time in my life, I confessed my California suicide attempt, and how Jesus Christ only weeks earlier, in my cell, had saved me from suicide with His call for me to "Help these men," meaning inmates with addictions. Two inmates stood up and gave their lives to the Lord, with the alter call by Don and Marg Baker, Christian ministers. When two officers oversaw the large number of inmates attending my testimony, one said, "I've never seen such interest! They must be giving something away free of charge!"

Three weeks later in the "Programs Building" I was invited to attend a function of community members, churches, corrections management and staff, and inmate representatives, of which I was one. We mingled and made small talk with people from the outside. But we inmate reps stuck together because it was more comfortable. Then, a major surprise! The deputy director, mentioning my name, and the Connection to Freedom program, invited me to speak. I felt the power of the Holy Spirit as I stood up to speak in front of the corrections/community audience of about twenty people, some by their smiles showing approval. I closed my testimony with "Remember Jesus Christ and remember, Connection to Freedom!"

On my last visit to the chapel by invitation from Don and Marg Baker, the ministers, I shared my testimony expressing my thanks to God and the inmates, the chapel staff, and others. I was asked to wait a few minutes before walking back to my seat. Several inmates stood up and one handed me a rolled-up paper. I opened the scroll to see what turned out to be well over thirty inmates' signatures, and various officers and program staff had also given their signatures. An example of the notes attached to those signatures was, "Thanks to Connection to Freedom for helping me. God helped me through you, Steve."

With a visit in my cell by an NA member, the man who had given the alcohol and drug seminar, and input from the manager of programs and services, I was invited to hold a Narcotics Anonymous meeting. I humbly accepted. Through this, I gained some valuable experience as chairperson. It was a great meeting with recovering addicts from the community. But the jail brought an end to the meeting when it was suspected that one of the community members of NA was "high" on drugs. I did not judge the addict who had a slip while in the NA meeting at the jail. My thought was he was too afraid to come to jail sober. In my own life, I was comfortable in jail. The following from the Lord as I read my bible, spoke to me clearly and made all the sense in the world to me:

"In this you greatly rejoice, though now for a little while, if need be, you have been grieved by various trials, that the genuineness of your faith, being much more precious than gold that perishes, though it is tested by fire, may be found to praise, honor, and glory at the revelation of Jesus Christ, who having not seen you love" (1 Peter 1:6–8).

Janet eventually brought the completed book back to the jail and left it for us. She had attached a note to the book, that said, "Well done you guys, keep up the good work!" The name Connection to Freedom was very well known to inmates. But, for reasons beyond my comprehension, I needed to re-read the letters written on my behalf for parole support. The letters were from a John Howard Society of Victoria Employment Counselor, the Director of Programs and Services for VIRCC, the Case Management Coordinator for VIRCC, an Elder with the Church of The Way Chapel Program. The following are excerpts from these letters:

"I have been working with Steve on his formatting and implementing of a very sound and productive group-- Connection to Freedom. I wish to assure anyone questioning Steve's sincerity in this change in his lifestyle, that he has convinced me and that I will assist him to the best of my abilities and resources". – Tejuanis "Butch" Cassidy.

"Mr. Bradley was singularly instrumental in leading the development of a program called 'Connection to Freedom' which started weekly counselling group sessions with up to fifteen inmates. This proved especially beneficial for some of the younger prisoners who were having problems adjusting to life in the institution."

"Mr. Bradley put together a hand-out called 'Connection to Freedom' which all members were given. He is at present working on another project which deals with a person while in custody and on the street."

"I have found him to be very sincere in his religious beliefs. Steve has enormous leadership abilities and has earned the respect of both prison staff and other inmates. On many occasions, I have advised newcomers to the jail system to seek out Steve for advice, and he has helped many inmates adapt to their surroundings."

I recalled my parole hearing: The board asked me whether I would blame "the devil" if I got into trouble and came back to jail again. My answer was, "It will be my fault if I come back to jail, and if God wants me to stay in jail, you won't grant my parole. This would just mean that He has more work for me to do in here." With strict stipulations, the board granted me parole to my brother's home. The board wrote that I had "seen the light" (God's vision for my life.)

Around December 15th, I was busy putting together my personal effects to vacate my cell in favor of paroled release to my brother's home. I began to worry about how the churches and Christian community were going to accept me. At that moment I remembered when I was in jail in 1982 and living in the West Wing Dorm at Wilkinson Road Jail. This is what happened: Inmates were giving a rough time to a young guy who was a Christian. He read his bible at night and in the daytime and inmates gave him a hard time for his preaching about Jesus Christ.

I don't know why I stood up for him but holding a wooden chair leg and waving it threateningly, I called out, "If you guys don't stop threatening that kid about his religion, come ahead if you think you can do something about it!" I remember how a woman from Western Community Baptist Church visited me and gave me a bible signed by her and her husband. They were the bible teachers of the young Christian guy. That same year, a couple of months later, I caught an inmate stealing from other inmates, and I lost it! I punched him in the head so hard that some blood hit the wall about six feet away. I lay on my bunk, trembling so hard I couldn't stop while flashes of red were all I could see. My own rage was the only thing in my life that frightened me. Suddenly, my memories of five years ago were lost, and I found myself back in 1987, the present.

When I was about to leave VIRCC on parole, inmates were wishing me well and thanking me for the help they had received. A First Nations guy asked me to take his and other stories in the Connection to Freedom book to help schools to help students stay away from booze and drugs and crime. "You'll be speaking in schools, Steve!" My French-Canadian friend who had given us our Connection to Freedom name, said, "Keep the meetings and the book going if you can, Steve. After all, the program started right here in this jail!"

Now, walking toward my freedom on parole, I felt lost without my inmate friends, unsure whether I should have applied for parole, and envious of the inmates I had come to know. They would have a comfortable Christmas. My Christmas would not be comfortable, I felt. Waiting for a taxi, while smoking my tenth cigarette since breakfast, I looked at my nicotine-stained fingers, feeling shame, and worrying about how the Christian community would look down on me for being a chain smoker. I could figure a way! I could smoke in the doorways, and at night nobody would be able to see me. I just needed to figure out a schedule so the Christians couldn't see me with my cigarettes! The taxi arrived.

As I glanced back at the castle-style building and two officers walking down the front steps, I was reminded of the too many times I was an inmate there when it was Oakalla Prison Farm -Vancouver Island Unit, Colquitz Gaol, Wilkinson Road Jail, and that was my second time at Vancouver Island Regional Correctional Centre. I had worked at the corrections camp "Lakeview," a branch of Wilkinson Road Jail, seventeen years ago, for possession of burglary tools.

As the Taxi drove through the open gate I remembered my jail term when guards carried rifles, and my mom's visit.

From where she sat mom could see past the iron gate when a guard was securing his rifle, and another was picking up a rifle for afternoon shift. I recall there was a place on the jail property called the Blue House, where some inmates, on weekend sentences were housed, and those close to parole or community release. I was housed there myself once.

Back then when mom visited me, she asked me, "Do the guards shoot real bullets or are they only warning pellets?" I thought back to a morning when the kitchen was annexed to the jail. Rolls of barbed wire were stretched out atop the fencing. Outside stood a guard holding a rifle. It was dark and early morning in the winter, and after breakfast we would be working on our individual gangs. I was on the farm gang or clearing the fields, I cannot rightly recall.

Since I started going to jail when I was not much more than 20, I had worked in the Taylor Shop, Clothes Change, and I was a tier cleaner and had janitorial duties with an electric floor polisher. I always tried to get a janitorial job when I was booked into the jails. Mom had asked me what my job was in prison. Until she jolted my brain with her questions, I had walked past a guard with a rifle, not giving it another thought. To me it was simply "us" and "them".

The taxi stopped at my brother's home as I lit another cigarette.

"On Parole"

It was not easy imposing myself on my youngest brother and his daughter at whose home I lived during parole. Being released at Christmas time was a test all by itself. It was hell not being able to drink but, of course, a shot of heroin would then follow, and I'd be on my way back to jail. I missed my friends at VIRCC, but Christmas 1987 soon became New Year's Day 1988, and thanks partly to twelve-step meetings, but mainly to my bible and prayer, I stayed clean and sober. I wrote letters to inmates, and I looked for employment using telephone book advertisements.

In the first week of 1988, having never stopped my jailhouse writings, I wrote piles of papers with which I planned at some point to make a much bigger Connection to Freedom book. I also penned the first pages of another idea for a book, one that might be used in schools with a non-religious format. Little did I know that this would become two books—The Way It Really Is and For Youth at Risk and In Conflict—and that they would help save two inmates' lives, one in New Brunswick and the other in South Dakota.

My niece encouraged me whenever she saw I was feeling depressed. "Keep writing, Uncle Steve," she said, "you'll help a lot of school kids one day!" This reminded me of the young First Nations inmate at VIRCC who had said, "You'll be speaking at high schools one day; take our stories with you!" My lack of self-worth would still not allow me to believe either of them, but their words kept me pushing on if only to see if schools would accept my book. I read the bible, searching for a way to quit cigarettes. I was hoping for a solution that was not too religious or complicated. I found nothing. But then I got stuck on a certain page.

I couldn't take my eyes off the words as if I were riveted to my New King James Version bible: "And whenever you stand praying, if you have anything against anyone, forgive him, that your Father in heaven may also forgive you your trespasses. But if you do not forgive, neither will your Father which is in heaven forgive your trespasses" (Mark 11:25–26 NKJV).

I spent most of that day meditating on "forgiveness." But I was smoking my foolish head off, coughing and spluttering as I prayed. Searching for the meaning buried deep within the two verses, I sensed the presence of God as profoundly as I had at VIRCC. I slept peacefully that night of February 15th, 1988. The next morning, I awoke and automatically reached for a cigarette. My brother in the bed next to me "lit up," so I inhaled deeply and coughed and wheezed as I had for far too many years. As smoke filled the room like a rolling fog, I watched the red-hot ash burn the end of my cigarette.

Suddenly I was overcome by a power that can only be described as from the Holy Spirit; then and there I put out my cigarette. At that moment, I understood the bible verses I had read the day before about "forgiveness," although I still couldn't understand how these "words" had removed my craving for cigarettes. That day, all day long, I had no desire for a cigarette. I was filled instead with a need to shout from the rooftops how prayer and God's word had set me free from cigarettes!

I knew that it was also my commitment as a believer to take this hope to others who were trapped in nicotine addiction. I could not share my testimony with many at my brother's home, so I decided to move downtown to work on the streets. I also knew I had to organize and hold Connection to Freedom meetings. I felt that a church would gladly provide us with a meeting space. After receiving my parole officer's permission and feeling it best for my brother and his daughter to get back to their routines, I rented a unit at the Upper Room Society. This was a street shelter and community kitchen with small units for rent.

Searching for Group Space

In Unit 4, my residence, I continued writing and met with fellow residents to talk about the Connection to Freedom meeting and ask if they would like to join. The more I shared with residents and others, most people I met, how Jesus Christ and God's word, the bible, had set me free from cigarettes, the stronger I felt spiritually, and the more people were drawn to me. As I had done the previous year at VIRCC with the Connection to Freedom book, my thought was to ask people who were in deep pain to share their life experiences while I wrote their stories. This method, God had shown me through my prayers, was bringing "inner healing" to the lonely and hurting, those without hope or a voice of their own. So, there it was! Adults helping themselves to heal with a focus, not on themselves but on youth at risk and high school students. This was the map, the vision if you like, that the Lord had quietly implanted in my spirit.

Janet, the volunteer who had typed our original book and brought it back to the jail, was now assisting me by telling her friends about Connection to Freedom. She was a great advocate for the meeting and the book and took it very seriously. All we needed now was a space to hold the meeting. I felt sure that a church would help by loaning us meeting space. I prayed hard and was in my bible looking for answers while in Unit 4. My concentration was on the scriptures and updating my daily journal when suddenly I wrote, "The worst problems in my life are alcohol and drugs. I chose to use them, nobody else chose for me. It was me!" The shock of my confession, like never in my life, made me lose my footing and I dropped to my knees in tears!

I started hanging around the "Open Door" which was around the corner from the "Upper Room" and met several men of the street. One man, Glenn, who was a fantastic artist, contributed his illustrations to our Connection to Freedom book. I continued to walk the street looking for possibilities for meeting space. I telephoned a church with my request for a meeting space. The secretary hung up abruptly. Once again after prayer and scripture had encouraged me, I reached out by phone to a different church. The response to me was, "We cannot have 'ex-felons' and 'drug users' walking our halls, and it would frighten our congregation!" I met a woman who offered me an area in the basement of a house.

Two helpers whose stories I had recorded in the Connection to Freedom book joined me in my search. Then a man from Toronto who said he had served time in Detroit and was formerly in the Canadian Army offered his kitchen for our meeting. But he didn't want anything to interfere with his "alcoholism," so I turned down his offer. It couldn't have worked. It didn't either; he came to my room drunk out of his mind. BK, a former Texas chain-gang prisoner, and Pete, who had been in prison in Kansas, suggested I get my story into the Times-Colonist newspaper to let the community know of our need for meeting space for our Connection to Freedom group. Prayerfully, I began to consider this idea. Several days later I went to the Times-Colonist.

I told the reporter who interviewed me twice, my background, and God's calling to start the Connection to Freedom meeting and the book. The interview ended with my telephone number. The heading of the article referred to "Ex-con finding a connection to freedom." I had clearly reached out to the Christian churches through my published testimony, and I was very excited. I believed that letters and telephone calls would begin to pour in. Not because it was my life, but because Christ had been glorified. I did not once doubt that I would be contacted by someone who believed that Jesus was and is the Great Redeemer, yes, even of convicts and ex-cons. I was still finishing my parole.

Sadly, there was no response. Days passed, weeks passed, and I was so disheartened that I began to wish I were back at the jail with my friends. I remembered when I asked a Christian counsellor to pray for me just after I moved from my brother's home to the Upper Room. The answer I received was: "I don't think you are going to make it, Steve. Alcohol and heroin are too powerful!" When I shared how the Lord had set me free from cigarettes, his response was, "You'll probably start smoking again!"

I took my recovery seriously, but I still could not shake off some memories of my years as a heroin addict. From sleepless nights to deep periods of sleep and terrible nightmares, it was always the same theme: Two guards would call my name: "Bradley, where are you?" Meanwhile, my shattered nerves were calling out to me, "Get yourself some heroin! Get some heroin! You need it!" I was in jail for burglary and the two guards had brought me some heroin. In my nightmare that is! One guard pushed a wheelbarrow with a large capsule of heroin in it and the other carried an intravenous needle as big as a garden shovel. "Come and get yourself some heroin!" They kept calling me! While fighting these demons from my past there was also a nagging in my brain for alcohol and heroin to give me some peace from the struggle known only too well by those who have struggled to give up cigarettes, alcohol, heroin, or opioids.

The worst rejection I would ever face in my life was in California one month before my nineteenth birthday. On July 4th, I was run over by a car. The driver and his passenger walked back to see what they had hit on the road. "Hey, it's a guy! Let's get out of here!" I heard them running and their car door slam shut! Tires squealed as they sped away leaving me to die! (I felt just as rejected by the Victoria churches and the Christian community.)

A young man from Saskatchewan, who was telling me his story for the Connection to Freedom book, suggested I apply to the Mustard Seed Street Church and Food Bank for space to hold our Connection to Freedom meetings. He said the church had a lot of good people, some from the street. The youth said, "They are letting NA meet there. So, they should let your bible-based recovery group have meetings there!" I decided to go to the Mustard Seed, but I was so disillusioned by the lack of response from other churches and the Christian community in general that I knew if this were another rejection, I would give up and return to alcohol, heroin, and opioids. I'm sure that God intervened when the Mustard Seed board of directors, known as the church council, granted that in the New Year, 1989, we could begin holding weekly meetings of Connection to Freedom in their outreach area.

I had moved from the Upper Room and after a couple of months of renting a room in Langford at Janet's house, I had taken an apartment in downtown Victoria, which was not a far walk from the Mustard Seed. So, I became a Food Bank volunteer Mondays, Wednesdays, and Fridays. Within a brief period, I was also attending the Mustard Seed Street Church. I received the loan of an office where I provided bible counselling to addicts and ex-offenders, and parolees, and corresponded with inmates near and far. Often, I shared our Connection to Freedom book with people in great need and offered to help some men and women of the street to write their own stories. I shared my testimony and invited prayer, but I did not push "religion." I encouraged instead a "relationship" with Jesus Christ. With an invitation to me from a program staff member there, I shared my testimony at the William Head Institution. Following my testimony, at the end of the class, inmates asked me how Connection to Freedom works, the format, and so on. Another invitation came from a recovery group at the prison, which I enjoyed very much when the inmate chair said, "Steve's program is something like ours, but it is Christian based." With a group member who was on parole from Matsqui Institution, a Christian, and my co-worker Bev, we reached out to two federal halfway houses, sharing the Lord with the house residents. We held an abbreviated form of our Connection to Freedom meeting at one of the houses. The other was strictly against "Christian programs"; it seemed to be more his personal views than those stipulated by that halfway house.

At the Mustard Seed, an argument broke out as to the purpose of the Connection to Freedom meeting. A federal parolee tried to take over the meeting. He thought it should mainly be to support parolees only, with glory to Jesus coming second. When I found myself becoming angry at this certain Connection to Freedom meeting, instead of losing my temper, I made a telephone call for advice.

Meeting Formats

Prayerfully, I telephoned Rev. Lewis of Emmanuel Baptist Church who was holding a weekly bible study at the Mustard Seed which I attended. Our conversation went something like this: "Hello, Reverend Hal. It's Steve, the guy with the Connection to Freedom meeting!" "Yes, what can I do for you, Steve?" he asked. "I'm worried about our meetings. There is a power struggle within the group to take charge of the meetings. I know I'm not supposed to feel angry and violent, but this is how I'm feeling. Do you have any suggestions for me?" "Read Matthew 4:19 in your bible and then pray and see if God will help you." "What is Matthew 4:19, Reverend Hal?" I asked, too lazy to reach for the bible in front of me. "Steve, read it for yourself. That is the point I'm making!" From that telephone conversation, prayerfully reading Matthew 4:19— "Follow Me, and I will make you fishers of men"—and seeking God's will daily, I understood the proper format for the Connection to Freedom meetings. From that time on, the format has not changed. The scripture is the glue that held our meetings together.

In early 1990, once I started opening our meetings with the explanation that we are God's group based on His word, the power struggle for leadership ended. Shortly after learning the format of the Connection to Freedom meetings, I can't remember who it was from the Mustard Seed Street Church who phoned me, but he invited me to join a small prayer group in the outreach area. It was led by Rev. Arthur Willis. I thought of every excuse to not attend as I had no intention of going. However, something was pushing me, my conscience perhaps, to attend. I had been playing Russian roulette by allowing a friend to drink his beer in front of me. There was a bottle in the fridge that he left behind. All day long I could not stop thinking about that bottle of beer and I was beginning to rationalize and justify how "one beer won't be a problem for me! That is if I promise myself that I won't have any more than one!" The Holy Spirit took me to the prayer group.

The Prayer Group

Seated in a circle were Gordy, Joanne, and me. I cannot recall who else was there, but I recall there were five or six of us altogether. That is how I remember it anyway. Rev. Arthur, then interim pastor for the Mustard Seed, told us: "I'm going to pass around a prayer stone and when the stone reaches each of you, take hold of it and bow your head and pray. Ask the Lord if there is anything in your life that He isn't pleased with and ask Him to reveal this to you." Two years earlier, when I was on parole, living with my brother and his daughter, I received two bible verses that God gave me through prayer. It spoke about "forgiveness." To paraphrase, the scripture revealed to me that when you are praying, if you have anything against anyone, forgive that person. Because if you don't forgive, the bible says, neither will God forgive your "trespasses."

At first, I could not grasp what this had to do with giving up cigarettes. But the next morning (February 16, 1988) the Lord, it seems, wanted to make a point, so He released me from my desire for cigarettes! So, there I was for two years a non-smoker at Rev. Arthur's prayer session holding onto the smooth, shiny prayer stone. I bowed my head and prayerfully asked the Lord if there was anything in my life that He was not pleased with.

Instantly, in my spirit, I saw the word "Forgive!" And as clear as if it had been a neon light in the darkness, a memory from my childhood flashed back.

I suffered debilitating asthma attacks. And being a shy introvert didn't help me when it came to making school friends. The doctor had done every treatment possible and always warned me about wearing a hat when it was raining, to avoid foggy days, and to participate in breathing classes at the local hospital. Because of my breathing challenges, I was unable to play sports with some neighborhood boys who were kicking a football. Embarrassed and feeling unworthy, I tried as hard as anyone to run the length of the field. I had even found a discarded pair of boots and had them on when mom called across the field, "He's not like you, boys! My son is sickly! You better send him home now!" I was feeling worthless amid the laughter from some of the boys, so I went home. In my bedroom, although I was brokenhearted, I refused to shed any tears.

One particularly cold and foggy morning when my asthma was close to being debilitating, I was at school when our class was given a surprising uplift. Our teacher's interpretation of some verses from her copy of the holy bible surprised me. This was not part of the school curriculum; it was something she did on her own each day before classes. Our teacher was a gentle-spirited woman who reminded me of my soft-spoken grandma whom I really loved. Imagining myself walking beside a bible character, such as the Apostle Paul, to me was a refuge from the storms of my asthma attacks and reality. In fact, learning about the bible was the driving force that I looked forward to every morning. I was inspired to attend Sunday school classes to learn more. Whether I was wheezing or having a good day, I enjoyed listening to the bible stories.

My daydreams were shattered one morning when at school some money went missing. Because the so-called "victim" sat in front of me all the students' eyes were on my area. My breathing became labored, and I felt my cheeks turn red with embarrassment. I wanted to climb under my desk, but I was too afraid to even move. Because of my shyness due to the asthma, some pupils saw me as a laughingstock. I could not imagine any pain worse than being made to look like the class clown. The grey-haired, gentle-spirited woman who was our teacher, pointed at me in front of the class and called me "thief!" My pain became worse, much worse. I had stolen nothing! But in that moment of sorrow, I felt deep resentment and walked away from God and any interest in her bible, and I even quit Sunday school, which until then I had attended every Sunday morning.

Our family's next move was to a coal mining village near Mansfield. Because of the polluted air, almost daily I found it difficult to breathe. But I wanted nothing to do with God or the bible, and I made a vow that I would never forgive my schoolteacher! I had burdened myself for thirty-five years carrying that unforgiveness as if it were an open wound that could not heal.

No sooner did I recognize this, when I stood before the Mustard Seed prayer group, confessed my sin of unforgiveness and forgave my schoolteacher. No sooner had I forgiven my teacher than I felt as if God was removing a piano-sized object from inside my flesh, and I knew then the Lord God had broken the chains of my addictions. Alcohol had lost its grip, heroin had lost its grip and so had other opioids.

The scripture that had set me free from cigarettes in 1988 and in 1990 released me from alcohol, heroin, and opioids was, and is, Mark 11:25–26 in my New King James Bible. Living 'one day at a time', as Matthew 6:34 tells us to do, and praying, gives me sobriety for which I thank God daily. Forgiveness is the key. As Christians, we do not have an option whether to forgive or not. In obedience to Christ, and in line with God's word, *we must forgive.*

Meetings Almost Ended!

For three months in the late nineties, I almost gave up the Connection to Freedom meetings. Here is that story: Since childhood, I could never express my feelings easily, and I believe this contributed to the breakup of an important relationship. My partner could never get me to talk about my feelings. I lost all confidence and was filled with self-pity. After my separation from her, my long-time friend Ross, and a couple, Allan, and Gloria, put me up and each stay was a blessing. Even the Salvation Army Street Shelter, as I look back, was a blessing from God. But first I had to suffer.

I felt lost and lonely. I moved into the shelter on a long weekend, which is never a good idea if you have a choice. I had felt miserable all day, and nothing could pull me out of the dumps. To make things even worse, another resident was shaking a pill bottle and talking with someone about his pills: oxycodone and codeine. On the other side of me was a resident drinking alcohol. I thought of how a drink, or a shot of heroin would ease the pain of my broken relationship. But these cravings were gone just as quickly as they had appeared. Then I heard the two residents again, and it was almost as if they had been hired to live on both sides of me expressly to deliver torment and temptation. I was so wrapped up in my own worries and woes that I had not held a Connection to Freedom meeting since my relationship had ended a couple of months earlier.

Now, in my decision to walk away from God and my faith, I started to write a letter. It was not aimed at anybody, but I just needed to see where I was emotionally. Perhaps it was about my relationship, but I couldn't be sure. I was teetering on the precipice of an abyss about letting go of my Connection to Freedom meetings and school talks and all these meant to my life. I was now seriously considering a shot of heroin. Indeed, I was about to set out searching for any opioids when, in my spirit, I suddenly heard: "Apprehend that for which you've been apprehended." I knew this was God speaking and that He was calling me to return to facilitating the Connection to Freedom meetings. I remembered God's call on my life in 1987 at VIRCC which had resulted in the founding of Connection to Freedom.

Our meeting was recorded in the unit officer's log of September 7th, 1987. Until that time, I had held several meetings basically as group discussions. These occurred when a few inmates began coming to my cell after Christ had changed me into a compassionate, confident, and peaceful person, at least in comparison to the madman, junkie, and alcoholic I had been before. It was not easy arranging the meeting for that night. We had no chairs, so I walked around Units C and D with permission and asked inmates if they were coming to the meeting. I collected the chairs from their cells. Each cell had a chair.

There was an area of Unit C that was a laundry and recreation room, and it had a ping pong table. I put a blanket over the table and net so the table would not get damaged. I had put a request in for coffee for our meeting, which was being held to vote on a name for our group. I received no reply from anyone about coffee, but fortunately, an inmate had some stashed in his cell and he gave it to us. I felt pleased as I heard inmates talking about our meeting. Finally, with me as the facilitator, thirteen of us sat down. It was early evening when the meeting began. I knew some inmates, but the rest were unfamiliar to me. On my left sat the big French-Canadian weightlifter who had suggested the name "Connection to Freedom." I was terrified of public speaking and had avoided it when I was in high school. Nevertheless, silently I prayed for God to help me and started by saying, "Thanks for coming, you guys! We're trying to get ourselves sober because we are tired of coming to jail. If you want the same thing, it's good to see you!" One guy became angry and started rattling on about society's problems and some government issues regarding drugs. Then another inmate spoke about his marijuana addiction, and another bellowed about legalizing cocaine and heroin. A fourth prisoner said something about wanting nothing to do with God. That was it!

I snapped! It wasn't so much anger that I felt as a bruised ego. The meeting had quickly gotten out of my control. Then, loudly, and sternly, I said, "Listen to me! If you don't stop trying to talk over each other, I'll climb over this table, and even though I may not be very big, I'll give you a shot in the head!" There was silence as I slammed my hand hard on the table! Then I heard somebody laughing and turned to my left to see it was the muscle-bound French-Canadian weightlifter who suggested our name. Angrily, I looked at him and said, "This means you too!" At this point God must have stepped in because there was a sudden calm as we voted to choose a name from sixteen inmates' suggestions, my choice being "Escape to Reality." It was unanimous. We inmates voted "Yes" for the name "Connection to Freedom."

After the meeting, I apologized to any prisoners I had offended with my attitude, explaining, except for NA, it was the first time I had ever spoken in a group. Their incredible response was that they thought I had done all right. Indeed, the unit officer's logbook for that evening described our meeting as "well-organized and orderly." This was the founding of Connection to Freedom. Men who had served time for murder, a man awaiting trial for bank robbery, another for trafficking in heroin, an ex-biker and two young First Nations inmates were among the first to come to my cell, building up to the founding meeting of Connection to Freedom.

God used the twelve inmates at our founding meeting as an example to show me, as I reflect these many years later, that we were His disciples. Christ in me was the group facilitator. Suddenly I was jarred from my heavy thoughts by the sound of clinking glasses and the smell of alcohol permeated my nostrils. I was in the street shelter but now feeling a lot stronger. The following week I held a meeting and, from that time on, in twenty-five years, never again have I forsaken the Connection to Freedom meetings or the needs of our group. And, after receiving pastoral advice about forgiveness and self-forgiveness, I was able to let my relationship go. Now, I feel no more pain, and through my daily God-given sobriety, I feel I am loved by Him. Thanks to the Salvation Army.

The stories in the following segments are about Connection to Freedom.

Janet's Story

I had not heard from Janet for many years, but on December 6, 2022, she phoned me. Apparently, she had tried to find me but did not have my address or phone number. I was blessed to learn how Janet caters meals to some seniors. I was happy to learn that all her family are "doing well." I remembered how in 1988 and 1989 Janet devoted many hours to help develop the Connection to Freedom book. Well, let me share with you how she helped not only me but VIRCC inmates as well. Here is her story:

Through a friend named Jane, I was introduced to the Connection to Freedom book almost ten months ago. She came to me and asked if I knew anyone who would do some typing for inmates of the VIRCC who had put a book together. I told her I would do it for them. As I was typing, I thought it was interesting reading and it was good that a book like this was coming from inmates. My brother had been in and out of jail for a long-time years ago. I thought if a book like this had been written a long time ago maybe my brother would have looked at his life and what he was doing with drugs and alcohol. I've seen what drugs and alcohol can do to a lot of people, especially friends, both of my brothers, and me. I lived through a lot with my brother. I watched what was happening to him. One day he was so bad that one of his friends came running into the kitchen and said to me, "Your brother is going under!"

I didn't know what to do because I'd never seen anyone overdose before. His friends tried to help but couldn't, so I phoned the ambulance! My brother almost died but was hooked up to a heart machine. He was in the hospital for two weeks. I watched the pain in my parents' faces, and there was nothing I could do but try to make my brother realize what he was doing to his family who loved him. My brother and I were very close, but I've always been on the other side of the street and wondering what was so great about being high or loaded all the time. It wasn't something I wanted in my life. But the people my brother knew had respect for me because I didn't bother them, and they never tried to push me into drugs.

One day Steve came over and told me that a guy on the street came to him with some drawings and asked if he could use them. Steve showed them to me. I thought they meant something, but what? I told Steve we should put the drawings on the floor so we could put them in order. We didn't have time to do much because it was late, and Steve would come over in the morning. Then we would put the book together.

When I woke up the next day and had coffee, I started looking at the testimonies, and poems. I would pick up one testimony and then a poem. Without realizing it the poems were going along with the testimonies. When I looked at the drawings Steve had brought, I saw they went with each chapter I was putting together. I had worked three straight months on the book with Steve. I hope with all my heart what prisoners (and street people) have done here will help you, whether you are young or older, to come to peace within yourselves. I know it has opened my life again with memories of what my brother had gone through, his friends, my friends, and others. Steve and I would like to thank everyone for their patience while waiting for the Connection to Freedom book.

It's been a long road of dealing with people's lives. We started with fifty-two pages (that were received from inmates at VIRCC) and now we're well over two hundred pages. If you have ever tried to write a book, you'll understand why it took us a year to put it together. It started with a suicide note (Steve's), and it grew to help people with their lives. I should know because it helped me in my life. I thank God, and Connection to Freedom for all it has done for me. I have met some of the people in this book. The unreal part is that some of the people I met—Jay, who just arrived from Ontario, John, from Fort Saskatchewan, and Ken, who was new to Victoria—came from out of the blue to tell their stories for the book, as Steve did the writing.

"Book Interviews"

These stories I collected mainly by interview on the streets of downtown Victoria and as written for the Connection to Freedom book, by inmates at the Vancouver Island Regional Correctional Centre.

"We had a meeting once a month in the Texas State Pen and the guy drove all the way from Houston to Huntsville. I was surprised that on August 3, 1988, to find out that the guy I was sitting next to in the Vancouver Island Regional Correctional Centre, was the one who gave our book its name."

"Over the years I lost my faith in God since I was abused as a child. At sixteen I was arrested in Havre Boucher, Nova Scotia. I had drunk too much and the RCMP drove up and informed me I was under arrest for intoxication in a Public Place. I was taken to Antigonish lock-up for forty-eight hours. I was sentenced to eighteen months in the Halifax Regional Correctional Centre for fraud related crimes. I feel eternally grateful for becoming a member of Connection to Freedom".

"I would like to get the problem I have off my chest. Connection to Freedom to me, is bettering yourself, for yourself, not the guy next to you. If I feel good about what I do, then why should I care about criticism."

"Here I was lying in the Essex County Jail. Three weeks in an 'isolation cell'. I didn't care if I lived or died. I had sunk to the bottom, at least, the bottom for me. I had a raging case of Infectious Hepatitis. I know one thing though I have an addiction and unless I allow the Lord into my heart to take control of my life, I will never make it. I strongly endorse what Connection to Freedom is doing in the jails and community."

"Last November I read Connection to Freedom while I was locked up in Wilkinson Road Jail. I felt good about the book. I am facing attempted murder trial in two weeks. I am giving my testimony to help myself and other people. This charge really woke me up."

"I am new to Victoria, but I was here no more than a few days when I heard of the Connection to Freedom book. In Brant County Jail I saw a guy slash his wrists with a razor blade and it scared me but not enough I guess because I ended up in the Mimico Correctional Centre in Toronto for Breaking and Entering". (This young man and I became close friends and in 2006, he joined me to speak at a six-week seminar for Claremont Secondary School students.)

Interviewing people with backgrounds like my own was not always easy but the result when each told his story to me, formed a friendship that was and is very special to me.

In 2005 I interviewed a man from Memphis, Tennessee, visiting Victoria. His girlfriend told me he was addicted to video games, and she asked what she might do to help him. Around the same time a homeless man who was addicted to Crystal Meth, crossed my path. He not only gave me permission to interview him for his story, but he also accepted my invitation and was my co-speaker at a high school. This was important because a 13-year-old schoolgirl had died from Ecstasy that was laced with Crystal Meth.

I had advised Jesus Christ as the answer for my interviewees. Both the Memphis video game "junkie" and the Victoria Crystal meth addict, have their stories, in two different books that I wrote and published in 2004, and a 2013, co-authorship with Aneil, now a Pastor with the Connection to Freedom Community Church in Duncan, BC. -author

Then you will call upon Me and go and pray to Me,
and I will listen to you. - Jeremiah 29:12

We became a non-profit

It was about 1995 when I applied for sole proprietorship for my work at the schools. In other words, I registered for this work, so I could become a business. I could use the money I earned from working with "youth at risk" to live on while facilitating Connection to Freedom meetings and outreaches. I ordered business cards and collected character references and support letters, so I was finally ready to proceed. Armed with my recently published books, The Way It Really Is and For Youth at Risk and In Conflict, I set out to make my presentations.

I reached out to people and organizations in the community that I thought might be willing to hire me or at least pay something for my services. Although I almost wore out my shoe leather, there was no response to my applications, telephone calls and letters. Very few did reply but not with offers of financial help, so I became discouraged. While feeling somewhat down on myself, however, I remembered the youths who were suffering. I also recalled my own youth and that was it! While still living on welfare, I decided I would help these young people, money, or no money, for pay or for free!

Very little came out of my sole proprietorship attempts, but seven years later, after being bombarded by suggestions that I seek non-profit status for Connection to Freedom meetings and outreach, I seriously began to consider that. Prayerfully, and with advice from several people such as church pastors I had met on my travels, I began to write the by-laws and constitution of Connection to Freedom's work. I was assisted by a small group of friends, including Kurt and Ross, as well as Garey who donated a ten-dollar typewriter. Using the hunt-and-peck method, I pounded the keys on that machine from morning to night until my fingertips were sore.

My proposed wording of "Christian support group for addicts and ex-offenders and a program for youth at risk" was refused. If the wording "youth at risk" was to be accepted, I was told, we would first have to go through a review by the government ministry responsible for children and families or perhaps it was the ministry responsible for youth. I cannot recall! So, I talked it over with Kurt, Ross, and others, and we prayed for God's will.

We decided against including the words "youth at risk." We stuck to a "Christian support group for addicts and ex-offenders." Ours was to be an organization registered with the government to work with adults. It was February 19, 2001, when, as a five-member board of directors with me listed as the founding member and contact person, "Connection to Freedom Jail and Street Outreach Society" was accepted. After some time, it was decided by the board that I would be the executive director and would be responsible for meetings, outreaches, and regular reports to the board. Finally, I would receive a regular salary.

Connection to Freedom House

At Connection to Freedom meetings, I encouraged the group to pray for a house for addicts. Whenever I shared my testimony in the community, I referred to our organization's project of a Connection to Freedom House. I received an invitation from the Western Community Baptist Church to share my testimony, and with permission, I invited three others to join me with their testimonies. Their prison backgrounds were Kent, Matsqui, and William Head Institution and my last sentence was spent at VIRCC. Before we surrendered our lives to Jesus Christ one man had suffered with alcohol, the next man from cocaine, our third Connection to Freedom group member had suffered from addiction to nicotine in cigarettes, and my addiction of many years was to alcohol and heroin, but through prayer and God's word, I was a non-smoker.

At the church, we believed that God answered our prayers when a member of the congregation stepped forward after our testimonies and donated a house. Just like kids on Christmas morning, all except me were rejoicing. To me, it seemed too good to be true. Sure enough, half an hour later the gift giver reclaimed her house. She confessed her mistake. Although we didn't recognize this as God's work, personally, I felt thoroughly embarrassed and ashamed. It occurred to me that none of us had sought scripture to confirm God's will that morning, but instead, we had raced blindly to the church to give our testimonies and ask for support for a "Christian" house. Two years passed and the vision of a Connection to Freedom house that had once burned brightly for several years had dimmed. But a telephone call revitalized my desire!

The caller was a person who with her husband was a generous supporter of our non-profit "Connection to Freedom Jail and Street Outreach Society." She asked, "Do you want the house in today's newspaper that is for sale? Could you use the house for a Connection to Freedom house?"

Our board of directors, as did I, the executive director, prayed and sought God's will. The board left it up to me. Meanwhile, we visited the house in question and found that it was about three doors away from the Victoria Methadone Clinic. "Steve, how fortunate," some people said. "If heroin addicts need help you can be reached even in the middle of the night!" I felt my ego was on stage taking a bow, but the time for turning the offer down had become much shorter.

Because God had used prayer and His word to free me from cigarettes and alcohol and heroin and opioid pain killers there was no doubt in my mind that He would answer my question: "Lord, is it your will that we accept the offer of a house?" I shared with our potential benefactors how God's calling on my life, was not a house but bible-based Connection to Freedom recovery meetings throughout the community.

"Therefore whoever hears these sayings of Mine, and does them, I will liken him to a wise man who built his house on the rock: and the rain descended, the floods came, and the winds blew and beat on that house; and it did not fall, for it was founded on the rock. But everyone who hears these sayings of Mine, and does not do them, will be like a foolish man who built his house on the sand: and the rain descended, the floods came, and the winds blew and beat on that house; and it fell. And great was its fall." (Matthew 7:24–28, NKJV)

The Methadone Clinic

I had over three years, created a Job Seeking Newsletter program to help Methadone Clinic clients. The Director of the Methadone Clinic had given Bev, my co-worker and I, permission to hold a workshop to help his clients. He paid rent for us on a room in a nearby vacant house and I had used an office at the Clinic to set up my word- processor. It was here where I put the final touches to my concept. My idea was to use a newsletter to help the Methadone Program men and women, to advertise their hobby crafts, artwork, poems, all creations that were saleable. Any monies that might come in would be given to the Methadone Clinic, to assist those clients in need, such as baby clothes, hygiene products, clothing etc.

Prior to holding my workshop Bev and I asked permission to speak with the clients. Twenty or more clients spoke with us. I too, had been on Methadone as maintenance years earlier as a heroin addict. Before Christ saved me, I had cheated and used heroin. I quit Methadone and stayed with heroin. My last fix was 1987, in jail.

I knew three Clinic clients, such as Benny. I'd known him since our teens. When Bev and I interviewed him, he called out in a boisterous manner, "I'm not religious like you, Steve, that's why I don't go to your Connection to Freedom meetings! I've been on Methadone for more than twenty years, and I don't plan on quitting either!"

The clients had talked amongst themselves and decided that Bev and I were there to try and take them off Methadone. Likely, the clients thought because Bev was a social service worker, we were working with the Welfare Office. They had no need to worry. This program was just me, knowing the harsh reality of their being without, trying to help them. Bev had agreed to assist me.

Two or three were interested in my Job Seeking Newsletter and attended our workshop. The format of my presentation was to let the clients know if they wanted to take part, Bev and I would send our newsletter out to the community of Greater Victoria, on their behalf. We encouraged them to write their poetry, write their stories, draw their pictures, and if they had hobbies, to create something. Any monies that came in they would receive it, or Bev and I would buy food, baby clothes, whatever was their need. "God's hand is in this" we told them.

We held two or three sessions, ending with just one person. We were willing to work with her, but she didn't show up at our last session. Was this a waste of our time? At first, I felt this was the case but gradually as the Director and I attended a forum at City Hall on "Drug Deaths in British Columbia", I understood why he and I had been drawn together in our Outreach Work.

So, I mailed our "Job Seeking Newsletter" to prisons, and a response from Matsqui Institution came from an inmate I had known at VIRCC, when I was there. He was writing a book, titled 'One Rainy Day' another response was a former inmate of Mimico Correctional Centre, in Toronto. "Thumbs Up!" was the title of his book that he had begun writing. And, prayerfully, I mailed the newsletter to the Aids Vancouver Island's Needle Exchange, Salvation Army, and Vancouver Island Regional Correctional Centre (VIRCC).

I received a phone call from the Deputy Director of the VIRCC. He knew me as a former inmate there, and of my transformation in Jesus Christ because he saw this with his own eyes. He asked me about Connection to Freedom meetings. "How many are you willing to help, one or two inmates?" "I will come for one!" was my reply. The result was my co-worker, a former Stony Mountain Prison inmate, a Christian, and I, spoke with about ten or eleven inmates, who were the Inmate Committee for all the units, and the Deputy Director. We left the Vancouver Island Regional Correctional Centre that day feeling confident that we would soon be helping the inmates with Connection to Freedom meetings.

Sadly, my co-worker relapsed and committed a serious crime that put an end to my hopes of getting Connection to Freedom meetings back into the VIRCC. Nevertheless, I supported him in court, and wrote to him for four years at William Head Institution. I supported him at his Parole Hearing.

It would not be until 2000 when I received a phone call from the man who was Deputy Director for Programs and Services, on behalf of the two Chaplains. "Will you come to VIRCC, to hold your Connection to Freedom meetings for the general population and protective custody inmates?" For the best part of a year, the meetings were held on a regular weekly basis. My co-worker was Kurt who had a sound knowledge of God's word. I thought back to the Connection to Freedom book and the page with the Job Seeking Newsletter, and how God had used it, in a mighty way to inspire the Deputy Director in 1988, to reach out to me, but not until 2000, was it God's perfect time.

I recall how a member of our Connection to Freedom group, a former William Head inmate, had written letters to William Head Institution to encourage them to stock Methadone in their medications for inmates. But from natural causes, he passed away, and we shall miss him. I recall the night in Wilkinson Road Jail when we heroin addicts were going through cold turkey withdrawals, and were issued by the doctor, methadone tablets. But only for inmates on the "Junkies Tier" as named by a guard.

The Director of the Methadone Clinic and I, and others, served food on lower Pandora Avenue, to people of the street. Only days before Victoria's 'Great Blizzard of '96'. Two years earlier we had attended the Chief Coroner's forum at Victoria City Hall, "Drug deaths in British Columbia." But the newsletter I sent to the Aids Vancouver Island's Needle Exchange was used by God to establish Connection to Freedom meetings, and outreach, at the Needle Exchange.

The Needle Exchange

I knew absolutely nothing about the AIDS virus that had taken the lives of so many in San Francisco in the seventies and eighties. I didn't know because I didn't want to think that the disease had come so close to touching my life. I shot heroin with a man I later found out had died from AIDS. But then in 1990 came a telephone call that pulled me into the world of AIDS. That telephone call was from John, a young man who stated that he was an ex-offender. He had served some jail time at VIRCC, apparently. He lived not far from downtown and asked me to visit, so I agreed to meet with him.

While I was drinking coffee with John at his kitchen table, the pale looking ex-con said, "I know you have helped people who were in prison. I got your name from one of your flyers. I'm gay; I use heroin and I'm dying from AIDS." I was shocked as I knew that AIDS was a killer disease and was infectious. "It's not that I'm scared of dying," John said. "It's just that I don't want to think about it. Do you have any volunteer work I can do?" He said he had heard I was writing a book for youth at risk on the dangers of drugs and alcohol and criminal activity. "I've got a typewriter, and I can type," he said. As the days passed, I visited John, bringing him some of my writings. Working on my book seemed to give him a measure of hope, and I believe I even saw some enthusiasm in him. But the last time I visited, before his landlord told me of his passing, I caught a glimpse of the young ex-offender's roommates. They were in various stages of HIV and AIDS.

I suddenly remembered, perhaps selfishly, how many times I had put myself at risk visiting this young man. Nine years later, never forgetting John, I received another telephone call related to AIDS. The coordinator of AIDS Vancouver Island's Needle Exchange asked me to hold our Connection to Freedom meetings at their street outreach service facility. I made her aware that we were a Christian support meeting for addicts and ex-offenders, parolees, and individuals awaiting trial or on probation. But she replied, "Melanie has told us how much you helped her when she was struggling with heroin. This is enough for us. If your program works, and we've heard good things, we would like to have your group here at the Needle Exchange."

In memory of John, the young man who had died of AIDS, I was moved to accept the coordinator's invitation. I thought about Melanie's support for us to hold meetings at the Needle Exchange. It seems that after I had been helping this girl who was a heroin addict through her many latenight telephone calls to my home, she had given us some good publicity. "Yes, our group will work with your clients," I answered. Our first Connection to Freedom meeting at the Needle Exchange, which included two people with AIDS, was co-facilitated by my friend Kurt. This meeting was also attended by a young man from Milano, Italy, who was studying professional photography. He wasn't an addict or an ex-con, but a friend of his had been murdered in a drug deal gone wrong and his body had been dumped. "I don't have much to offer," the young photographer said in his broken English, "but anything I can do to help prevent another murder, I will do it!"

The Needle Exchange had a heavy atmosphere and spiritually was the darkest place in the city. For example, a man who was a hard-core heroin addict sat in our support group one night and said to me, "I'm not ready to give up heroin yet, but" as he pulled from his coat sleeve a knife "I'll tell you something Steve: somebody isn't getting his throat cut tonight. And he can thank your Connection to Freedom group for that because I've been listening to your stories. Will you hold this knife for me?" I took the blade and later turned it over to the Needle Exchange staff.

Into our second or third year, about 2000 or 2001, with much prayer support and help from Ross, the social worker, Reima-Lee, Kurt and Shirley Slater and other group members, I telephoned a dozen church pastors and invited them to come and meet our group members at the Needle Exchange. We hoped to have each pastor or leader go back to their church congregation or assembly and encourage them to help the addicts and the poor on our streets.

Among the churches and Christian ministries that responded favorably were the "Villa" house church, The Mustard Seed Street Church, Chinese Pentecostal Church through Deacon Joseph, Trinity Christian Centre, Victoria Harvest, Oak Bay Gospel Assembly, St. Stephens Anglican Church, Pacific Rim Alliance, Four Square Gospel, Cadboro Bay United Church,

Cliff Power, Rev. Gareth Evans, Rev. Arthur Willis, and Kenneth Copeland Ministries donated bibles. (Half the donation was given to the chaplains at VIRCC). Some promises were made and kept, so we were blessed. For some church leaders, it was the very first time they had met addicts who were high on heroin, crack cocaine, crystal meth or various opioids.

We considered the Needle Exchange clients as our "family." We had met with them, taught them the bible, and received their written stories to help high school students and thanks to Shirley Slater and her daughter who read scripture each week, we of the Connection to Freedom meeting were kept on our toes as far as the bible. I was blessed when God touched the life of Shirley's son.

During our beginnings at the Commercial Alley Needle Exchange, we had borrowed their mailing address. Letters were handed to me by their staff when we entered for the night's outreach and Connection to Freedom meeting. One envelope that stands out in my mind was from an inmate in California. He was reaching out to our group, asking for our prayers not only for himself but also for his cellmate. The prison was at Kern Valley. I was immediately drawn to this letter by my hospitalization in 1965 at Kern County General Hospital. It turned out that a member of our group at the Needle Exchange had served time at California's "Pelican Bay" State Prison. A man whose prison background was California County jails and Calexico, a federal prison, on the Mexico/US border (I had supported his parole at the Vancouver Island Regional Correctional Centre).

Our Connection to Freedom meetings and related outreach were supported with regular weekly sandwich plates, and Thanksgiving and Christmas dinners, donated by Dr. Douglas Hamm and his wife Jane who was a teacher. Several University of Victoria students, Bart and Gloria, and Geoff and Leanne also helped, along with Moji and family, who later donated and wrapped gifts for the street community. Aneil would help with the gift wrapping, The Mustard Seed Food Bank contributed cups of soups. My mother (who passed in 2022), Joel, Micky my nephew and niece, and her children, were volunteers on two occasions. Kerri and her children were a big help. We were at the Needle Exchange almost six years, during which time, after a year's internship, through the Mustard Seed Street Church, I had become a chaplain with the Baptist Churches of Western Canada.

Prison Ministry at VIRCC

In 2000 the chaplains at VIRCC invited me to hold regular weekly meetings of Connection to Freedom, for the general population and protective custody inmates. Before my life was transformed by Jesus Christ when I was desperate and nearing suicide, I too was a VIRCC inmate. However, Kurt, my co-facilitator, was not. In fact, he had never been in jail. But the importance of the meetings was God's word, and Kurt certainly knew his bible. After six months of meetings, which the chaplains called a "Christian support group for inmates with addictions," sadly, Kurt was diagnosed with cancer and was hospitalized. As I was facilitating regular weekly meetings at Aids Vancouver Island's Needle Exchange, as well as others, the question was, did I think I could continue the meetings by myself? Prayerfully, I sought the Lord. He revealed that I should continue and, in prayers, remember Kurt and his family.

For the next six months, two meetings once weekly, I arrived at the VIRCC, submitted to the search for contraband, and received my electronic security alarm which I fitted in my top shirt pocket. I then crossed the courtyard to the door of the "Programs Building" and after identifying myself and the program I represented, Control allowed me to continue to the chapel. Once seated, I glanced over my prepared bible message as Control announced my arrival at the VIRCC: "Connection to Freedom meeting in the chapel!" The announcement assured me that it was 7:00 p.m. and other than those asleep or engrossed in something else, VIRCC inmates had heard the announcement.

Prayerfully I waited to hear the inmate group running up the steps. For the next hour it would be the inmates, and me. In my shirt pocket I had a security alarm, should violence break out. I was not afraid of any inmates, but the security alarm was necessary, for me to hold Connection to Freedom meetings at the VIRCC. I heard the "Programs" door open, quickly checked the room which was used for Chapel on Sundays. I had enough bibles.

With looks on their faces that revealed anger, frustration, or laughter, I knew that through my instruction and our prayers, the Lord would settle us all down. The attendance was usually a handful but had been as low as one and as high as fourteen. Some were awaiting trial, others awaiting transfer to federal penitentiaries, and as I had been in 1987, for attempted robbery of a pharmacy, inmates were sentenced and serving their time at VIRCC.

At the end of our general population's Connection to Freedom meeting in the chapel, I was preparing to leave, cross the courtyard, and ride the elevator to my next inmate group, protective custody. But there was urgency in one inmate's voice that made me listen. He asked if there was a Connection to Freedom meeting available to him at the penitentiary he was being sent to on the mainland. The inmate said he wanted to learn more because this night when I told the inmate group that the Holy Spirit was making me smile and others smile as well, he was struck with the desire "to know more about God."

Prior to his being transported by plane to his designated penitentiary, through the Lord I stayed in touch with him by telephone, and as I had several times, I shared my testimony. Prayerfully, I invited him to receive Jesus Christ. As I waited for his response, I was reminded of the support I had given by attending his final court hearing and sentencing.

Answering his questions over the telephone with assurances and a bible verse, Hebrews 13:3, I knew he was waiting, perhaps a last-minute regret, but he confessed and repented of his sins, including his satanic belief, and in tears, the man invited Jesus Christ into his life. Silently, giving glory to the Lord, God gives the increase, not I, and knowing that I would be sending him letters of assurance, with a smile and feeling God's blessing, I hung up the telephone.

The second blessing was an inmate who, I'll be honest, I didn't think was paying attention when I was reading the bible or other inmates were praying. One evening after holding a Connection to Freedom meeting with general population inmates, I crossed the courtyard and had just stepped out of the elevator to the protective custody group when, before reaching the meeting room, I met the inmate who, let's just say, I had believed less likely to succeed.

The inmates in protective custody pointed to a man who they said was a serial killer. I believe I had seen a TV news item about him. He attended every one of the Connection to Freedom meetings, was quiet, but did participate in God's word, and prayer.

Humbly, another inmate shared how, since our last Connection to Freedom meeting, while praying and reading his bible, God's Spirit had inspired him to give his life to Jesus Christ. There was a definite excitement in him and a glow in his face and a sparkle in his eyes. I was overwhelmed with happiness for the young man and ashamed of my wrongful feelings about him, for putting God in a box.

Prior to my ending the Connection to Freedom meetings at the Vancouver Island Regional Correctional Centre, inmates asked me to tell them about my life as a heroin addict. I told them my story, or rather, shared my testimony as follows:

When I was one month away from my nineteenth birthday, homeless, I attempted suicide. I was run over by a car heading for Bakersfield. I was battered and broken, and bloody, on the desert road, two miles west of Inyokern, according to the newspaper, 'The Bakersfield Californian'. My hospital pain treatments were injections of morphine, given to me at Ridgecrest Community Hospital, Kern County General Hospital, and after Air Ambulance to Victoria, the Royal Jubilee Hospital. I left the hospital as a twenty-year-old morphine addict. Unable to find morphine on the street, in downtown Vancouver, at twenty- three, I injected heroin. This drug has similar chemical properties to morphine but is three times as potent.

A year after my first fix of heroin, which was on Rupert Street in Vancouver, I was lying on a filthy mattress in a bare room with ugly velvet curtains in Victoria. I sniffled, the sure sign my body lacked the heroin it needed just to feel normal. I was half asleep when "Crash!" the front door splintered. Part of the dining room wall fell. RCMP and Saanich cops were all over the place. I was dealing heroin out of a house just off Burnside. But I was sick because I couldn't find a vein and I kept missing. Blood was running down my arm. I was getting frustrated, and my arms were cramping. Before I could get my act together, a very angry cop was checking my arm for tracks and then stormed through my room. Panic and instinct had caused me to let fly of the needle before he saw me. Within minutes, the cop was violently shaking my curtains as if looking for a winning lottery ticket.

Meanwhile, I was trembling with cold-turkey withdrawal. I didn't have time to punch the needle into my aching vein. The angry man of the law shouted at me: "You're going to prison as soon as we find some dope in this house! And we know it's here!" I flashed to the needle that I hadn't heard land when I let it fly. Did they find it?

Meanwhile, I could hear other RCMP acting like stormtroopers ripping our house apart, choking my partner, and insulting my lady. I didn't care about ANYTHING! I was sick and my body was screaming out for a fix of heroin! My welfare cheque was coming this day and I wondered if these cops were going to grab it like they had done to other junkies in the city. I managed on wobbly knees to stand up as they charged out to their cars furious after they found no dope.

Peeking through the curtains, as the last car drove away, a strange sensation overtook me when I heard the needle hit the floor with a gentle "click." All I did was look through the curtains when the needle was dislodged. The cop had shaken my curtains violently but was unable to dislodge my needle. I injected the needle of heroin, and my head dropped to my chest, and I began to scratch. It was good dope! I nodded for about a half hour. It was the first time in a long time that I had gotten any kind of break! For a split second in my mind was the God of my childhood. With the RCMP missing my needle, which had heroin in it, I escaped prison for sure!

My welfare cheque arrived! I scored some heroin for my lady and me. She used most of her cheque on heroin. Then came the day I was so sick; all I could do was sprawl across the bed. I sent my lady out to hustle me up a fix. I looked around the room and thought to myself, all I own is this cheap TV which my lady had left on to keep me company, a leather jacket, and my gun. There in that moment of realization, I even thought about giving up heroin and going on the methadone program. Then I heard, "Hi, honey I'm back! I got some good stuff, and you'll love this!"

Two and a half months later, I was hired by a guy who had been robbed of his heroin stash. The guy who was robbed paid me four hundred dollars to take care of a rip-off artist. But it was dark, I mean pitch black! Taking dead aim, so I thought, I squeezed the trigger. The hills echoed with a loud explosion. The rip-off artist's pleading made it obvious I had missed my aim. "Click." The rifle was empty! Through a rush of adrenaline, I ran to the car to get more shells! I had told my partner to bring a box of shells. "Sorry, Steve, there are no more, the box is empty! I don't know how this happened!" Again, from a place I did not understand, I guess some call it "getting a break in life" or like that, I was spared from a probable murder charge. The rip-off artist I heard, paid his drug debt, and left Victoria.

I went to Victoria's first recovery house for heroin addicts, but it was a big joke. For the price of my welfare cheque, I was given a room with a bed and dresser. The top dresser drawer had 180 methadone pills in it. This was the "gimmick." Most of the junkies I knew ended up there just to use the methadone pills when the city was "dry"—no heroin!

My recovery, believe it or not, came when I hit rock bottom in my cell in VIRCC and on August 29, 1987, I called out, "God, if you are real, I need your help! I've destroyed my life and I've done it by myself!" That which followed from God has brought me back to this jail to help you inmates. By sharing the dark side of my life, which the inmate groups could relate to, but ending with an invitation to Jesus Christ, brought the Lord's credibility.

I recall a man who hardly missed a Connection to Freedom meeting who was said by his fellow inmates to be "a serial killer", and I remember the tears in the eyes of a gang member, and further spiritual curiosity in a man charged with murder, and a long-time federal prisoner who was "a bank robber" and "an animal lover". It was not easy giving up Connection to Freedom meetings at the VIRCC, but after I sought the Lord about it, I was confident that it was His time for me to "let go of the jail meetings."

That same year, Centennial United Church hosted our annual Connection to Freedom Benefit Concert. In support of the meetings and their participation by invitation, pastors of Victoria's churches, assemblies, and ministries, showed up and gave bible readings. The pastors and others encouraged me to also share God's word with the audience. Prayerfully, I felt the Holy Spirit guide me: "And you shall not glean your vineyard, nor shall you gather every grape of your vineyard; you shall leave them for the poor and the stranger: I am the Lord your God" (Leviticus 19:10).

Contributing to the benefit concert was a group of musicians and praise and worship singers. High in the Holy Spirit, smiling, I went to talk with the volunteer door man. Who was standing at the front door of the church? A man who, when he was an inmate, attended our Connection to Freedom meeting, and gave his life to the Lord.

Note: It was great to see Kurt at the concert, he was on the mend I heard, and a guy from Duncan who sometimes attended our Connection to Freedom meeting that we held thanks to room space loaned by Centennial United Church. Another Duncan resident, a woman, always had a joyous spirit, no matter the problem. She had attended Connection to Freedom meetings at Needle Exchange, Manchester House, The Mustard Seed, and twice at Our Place. -author

Homeless Man Finds Hope!

When I first met with a desperate man who was homeless, I learned more about the power of God. This man who was suffering from his addictions, became a member of our Christian addiction's recovery meeting, Connection to Freedom, thanks to space provided by Centennial United Church.

But I was first introduced to him in our meeting held by invitation from AIDS Vancouver Island's Needle Exchange. In the beginning, with anyone who reached out to him, he always showed his anger. He had been kicked out of several places, including the Needle Exchange, because some people were afraid of his angry outbursts.

I remembered my own periods of homelessness in Vancouver, Victoria and Trona, California, and how I was driven to attempt suicide. The homeless man talked about how miserable and desperate he was, and I began to worry that he might be thinking of suicide. But strange as it may seem, the homeless man started to pray with our group. We held a small group with space provided by Our Place. My friend, the angry man, began asking for a bible, which we gladly gave him. But only when he came to our meeting at Centennial United did, he hit rock bottom in his addiction. He began to walk to our group from his Beacon Hill Park "home."

Even in the howling winds and miserable rain, he showed up, sometimes soaked to the skin. God, in all situations, including homelessness, was in his life. That was becoming evident in our Connection to Freedom meeting fellowship. As the group facilitator, with Christ as my leader, I was often silently in prayer. The homeless man, whose residence was no more than a bushy area in Beacon Hill Park, after several months, said he was touched by the Lord.

I began to speak with him away from our group, sharing bible passages. He found the bible, even in his homelessness, encouraged him to not give up. The Lord blessed him when a member of our meeting, our piano player, offered him accommodation. She had opened the door for a miracle to happen. Soon after he found himself an apartment. When he shared this at a Connection to Freedom meeting, I sensed a group sigh of "relief!"

Hope on Pandora Avenue

On August 8, 1988, I was going to kill myself. I had been turned down by treatment centres, and my wife refused to help me anymore. I am a born alcoholic and I'm addicted to drugs. I am thirty-four and I've spent about twelve years in prison. I've seen inmates slash their wrists. I've seen them give up on life and hang themselves. I've seen inmates stab each other when hate was so thick you could taste it. Because of my emotional scars, I didn't really trust myself or care what happened to me. Drugs and alcohol became my God.

I shot speed at twelve years old, and up until I was twenty-two, I shot MDA and heroin and prescription drugs (opioids). I spent four years in Stony Mountain Penitentiary for smashing a hole in the side of a Winnipeg church. I broke into the safe, and the funniest part of all, as stoned as I was, knowing that the police were on their way and hearing the alarm go off, I sat down and asked the Lord for forgiveness. And He has been working on me ever since. As a matter of fact, He has been working overtime on me.

Today is August 9th, and I have found a reason to live by a miracle. I was walking up Pandora Avenue, and I kept running into people I used to do drugs with, but somehow, I managed to keep walking. I didn't know where I was going or why, but suddenly, I looked up and there was the Upper Room. The Lord had directed me to Steve Bradley who lived there. I know this was a miracle because about two years ago, Steve and I and Arnie, who later died of an overdose, were shooting heroin into our veins. There was no stopping us until the Lord put marriage before me and prison before Steve.

I have been a Christian since I was six years old but my addictions to alcohol and drugs overpowered me. My first jail was at Burtch Industrial Reformatory for stealing to support my drug habit. If there had been a Connection to Freedom book available to me in the Stony Mountain Penitentiary, I would have had a better chance at making something of my life instead of my destroying it.

Matsqui Parole Hearing

I had been counseling with an ex-prisoner when my phone rang. When I hung up, after having a conversation I thought about the phone call and began to consider the situation and the need. This wasn't the first time an inmate had asked for parole support. But something about this time was different than when I attended parole hearings at VIRCC, and William Head institution. I guess the difference was that I had been corresponding with this inmate at California prisons, and our Connection to Freedom group had been praying for him. I had known this man for years, but the difference now was that I was a Chaplain with the Baptist Churches of Western Canada. I had planned through the John Howard Society of Victoria, to stay at their John Howard House in Abbotsford, near the Matsqui Institution.

I had taken the ferry from Victoria to Vancouver by bus feeling confident after my prayers that morning. As the Abbotsford Bus pulled out of the Vancouver Bus Depot, I was focused on the upcoming Parole Hearing at the Matsqui Institution, and the John Howard House where I had arranged to stay. But, unbeknown to me this parole hearing was going to be more of a challenge than I had planned for. Not with the Parole Board, or the parole candidate, but, well, let me explain.

I made a trip to the prison to ask a correctional officer where the John Howard House was. It was as if I wasn't meant to have a comfortable trip. First, my travel had to be by taxi and my budget was very low. The correctional officers of Matsqui Institution had no idea where the House was. I walked the streets up and down two or three times then I went to the Police Station (to be honest, I was willing to sleep in one of their cells), but they pointed me in the direction of the Salvation Army. Nobody, and I mean nobody, knew where the John Howard House was!

It was very late, and I was exhausted from miles of wearing out my shoe leather. The parole candidate will never know the misery I went through to help him. Finally, I phoned the John Howard Society as a server at a coffee shop suggested and took a taxi to the John Howard House. That night I slept like a log. The next day at the Matsqui Institution, I attended the Parole Hearing.

I remembered the California prisons that I had written to him and when it was my time to speak, I said, "I have known this man (no name) for years, and I know what really makes him tick. All we see is the muscle-bound inmate with the tattoos. I believe his body; he has shaped to keep people away from him. What I mean is his body is a shell that has a frightened child hiding inside. If you give him a chance, I will do all I can to help him to help himself."

I was allowed to meet with the former California inmate who was now incarcerated at the Matsqui Institution. We had a laugh at my trying to find the John Howard House, and coming to the prison three times, to ask the night correctional staff where the House was. We talked about his old cellmate in the US who had transferred to Corcoran State Prison. I'll be honest with you I wasn't sure this parole candidate was going to be granted parole.

But I asked him about his plans, and I remembered that he had said to me, earlier, "I am an addict, and I will become religious if that's what it takes. I'll go to Connection to Freedom meetings, if I get out!" I asked him where he might stay, and he referred to the Salvation Army in Victoria. He went to the washroom then, and I wondered if I was doing the right thing by supporting his parole. But, because I had prayed about coming to the Parole Hearing, at Matsqui, I felt, let me say, confident in the Lord. We returned to the Parole Hearing and with strict stipulations the inmate was granted a Parole.

On the way back to Victoria by ferry, I thanked God and realized that not all our prayers are answered the way we think they should be. But He has a purpose that may be unclear to us. We need to step out in faith, no matter the challenges (Hebrews 11:1).

A New Brunswick inmate

When I first started writing to a certain Dorchester Penitentiary, New Brunswick, inmate, it was in response to his letter that I received weeks earlier. At that time, I had office space, a telephone, and mailing address, on loan from the Mustard Seed Street Church, on lower Pandora Avenue, in Victoria. The church also loaned me outreach space for Connection to Freedom meetings.

The Dorchester Pen inmate whose name I will keep confidential had written me a very disturbing letter with reference to him feeling suicidal. Before answering his letter and sending it, I prayed, sought scripture, and as I had with other inmate letters of sheer hopelessness, I encouraged him to write his story, not for himself, or me, but to help youth at risk. I had used this method, which I believed was God sent, with a young Lakota Sioux inmate at the South Dakota State Penitentiary.

So, to help the New Brunswick inmate whom I would write to for at least three years, I prayed for him, shared scripture with him, and focused in my letters on his writing his testimony. His reply made mention of his interest in Bible College, after his release. The prison Chaplain was a great help toward this goal. Not only that but the inmate, my pen pal, sent me photos of his young wife, and their marriage at the prison. I was blessed to see their smiling faces.

A Matsqui inmate had in his letter expressed "feeling severely depressed". So, I sought the Lord, scripture, and as he was not a Christian, I asked God, how I could help the man. So, once again, though many years later than the New Brunswick inmate, I encouraged him to write his story not for himself, but to help 'youth at risk'. He wrote a few stories about why kids should avoid cocaine. I was so impressed with his sincere effort to help others, that I invited him to suggest a title for one of my books. He said, in one of his many letters, "The Way It Really Is". My second book which was similar content, a suggestion from my street outreach, "For Youth at Risk and in Conflict".

I donated a copy of each to my friends, Ben and Germaine Vivian at California's Ironwood Prison, and a copy of each book went to the

Principal at a 100 Mile House high school. His comments by phone were: "Well done! Keep up the good work!" But a School Teacher in Prince Edward Island, who had received the two books, wrote to me.

"Thank you for the books but they are too real for our students." From Ottawa came a letter from the National Library of Canada, and to comply I sent them a copy of each book for their files. In 1994, and 1995, they were registered. Then came a letter of request from the Windsor Public Library in Ontario. I sent them a copy of "The Way It Really Is" and "For Youth at Risk and in Conflict".

Sometime later, I received a telephone call from an inmate, my co-worker Bev, and I had supported at his Recovery Centre up Island. However, he was in jail now: "Hello", I said. "Steve, I found one of your books here! The front cover is torn but I read it! I know some of the guys in there!"

"Hey man, keep up the good work, you're helping a lot of guys with your books!"

I remembered my friend, the Dorchester Penitentiary inmate, and I believe I heard he was attending Bible College. That New Brunswick inmate through the Lord, sure turned his life around.

Texas "chain-gang!"

Huntsville, Texas is where the main prison was, and we called it "The Walls." There were guys in there doing twenty years for possessing a cap of heroin. There were five other prisons on farms when I was there. It was a lousy fluke how I got caught. I'd been dealing 'weed' for years and thought of it as a business. Like, I wasn't laughing at the system or trying to beat the system. It's just what I did, you know. I thought I had it made but then I got pulled over by this West Texas Sheriff, I had the door panels and trunk stuffed with marijuana. There were twenty pounds in all. My lawyer told me I would get probation because it was my first offense, and because I was a Canadian, I might get a break. What dealing marijuana cost me was three years of hard labor on a chain gang for the Texas State Penitentiary system.

After work detail we had to strip off our dirty prison clothes and wait naked until we got into a shower and got clean clothes. Those Texas winters can be hell, but the summers can get up to 120 degrees. I picked cotton in boiling summer heat. One time I was working in a swamp up to my knees and I was bitten by a water moccasin. That's a snake that is deadly poisonous and can kill you. The 'high rider' which meant 'a guard on horseback', called for a 'taxi' which meant, 'a medical guy' back at the prison. I was given a shot to counteract the poison and got one day off work. Believe me, this was hard labor. I was as sick as a dog when I went back to the work gang.

Fifteen miles from the Texas border I bought marijuana and sold it back in Canada for a profit. None of it was worth my prison sentence in Huntsville. As I am flashing back, I can remember this guy who had been awaiting trial for a few months. He was put on the chain gang to work with a hoe. They called a hoe, an 'aggie' in prison talk down there. He fainted because of the heat, and I tried to pick him up, but the 'high rider' (the guard on horseback) told me to leave him alone. When a guy 'fell out' (dropped to the ground and wouldn't get up) he was sent to 'the hole' (a cell with nothing in it that was used for punishment).

I got greedy like everybody else who sells drugs, and I was taught a lesson I'll never forget. My sentence was three years chained to about nineteen other guys. It would be a good idea to get this Connection to Freedom book into the Texas Penitentiary system. I think it could help. I find it hard to talk at a meeting and I don't know how to write that well.

It doesn't matter how many guys show up for a meeting. We had a meeting once a month in the Texas State Pen. I went just to get four days off work detail. The guy who did the program drove all the way from Houston to Huntsville (about eighty miles). I can't remember his name but in him, I found a glimmer of hope. I can't really explain how it helped me. But it eased my prison time. That man made me feel good inside. Unless you have done jail time you might not understand. I believe there is a God up there, I just don't understand the teachings of the bible.

I want to thank the Connection to Freedom people those in prisons, and those on the outside. BK

"Remember the prisoners as if chained with them..." Hebrews 13:3

Hope in South Dakota Pen

A woman named Lois from Oka, Quebec, contacted me by letter with a request that I offer help to a young man, a Lakota Sioux, at the South Dakota State Penitentiary. I reached out to him by letter. His response was filled with depression and hopelessness, with a mention of suicide. As I had helped other inmates, in my next letter, I invited him to write his story, not for his sake but to help others, specifically, youth at risk. This seemed to lighten his load as he concentrated on helping others. But this didn't happen overnight because I corresponded with him for almost three years.

Knowing I was a Christian, he sent me a copy of the Lord's Prayer in his own language. But the day he sent me a photograph of he and his wife, after getting married in the prison, I knew by their smiles, in a photograph, that my understanding of God, had become a little clearer. I had learned about his mother and racial discrimination, and how she had suffered with her son in prison. But with his wedding, I know in my heart that in her own way, she was rejoicing.

Years later by invitation I held an eight-week life skills workshop for the secondary students at the Lauwelnew Tribal School in Saanich. As I shared my story with them, I was very much reminded of my South Dakota pen pal, and the hope he found at the bottom of his pit. With my last class at the Tribal school a newspaper reporter came to document my closing words. She reported that I was close to tears, as I said, goodbye. The students you see had made me their own "Thank You" cards.

Not long after I held a six-week workshop for a group of residents of the Victoria Youth Custody Centre. During which I shared two of my own experiences:

With two other guys I was busted on Cook Street while on our way to rob a jewelry store. We were charged with possession of burglary tools. A cop had testified against me when the judge asked, "Why did you follow their car officer?" His answer, "Because of the way the defendant Bradley looked at me, your Honor." My two co-defendants were sent to Oakalla Prison in Burnaby, and I was sent to the Wilkinson Road Jail in Saanich. The next experience followed.

I felt very ill and confused and very hot in my jacket, that I wanted to rip off me. They handcuffed me and the next thing I remember is I'm sitting in the hospital intake area listening to the tapping of a typewriter. The intake nurse cautioned the guards not to leave me alone with her. She asked questions of one of the guards: "Inmate's name and number? Date of birth? What is the name of the jail where the inmate is from?" The two guards couldn't agree on the name of the institution. One answered "Oakalla Prison Farm- Vancouver Island Unit". She typed it in her report.

These shared experiences seemed to put the young offenders' suspicious natures to rest. As a closing, the group thanked me with a Certificate signed by them all. Of course, I refrained from shedding any tears. I did not refrain from declaring my faith in Jesus Christ, that I had received at the point of suicide at 41 years old, in my cell at the Vancouver Island Regional Correctional Centre. A former East Vancouver youth gang member asked for and received my support. Together we shared our stories for The News Group newspapers, who did a large article on Youth Gangs, and Violence. But never will I forget my young South Dakota friend.

Probation Officer's OK

When Benny, an old friend, and I were much younger, and in trouble, my Victoria probation officer strongly suggested I take him with me, if I wanted his OK to go to Edmonton. So, as if I were babysitting him, Benny and I arrived in Alberta's Capital. He disappeared half an hour after we stepped off the bus. Understandable since we had landed in the howling winds of a blizzard. Our clothing was raincoats suited to the Victoria weather but not the middle of an Alberta winter. I found him in a coffee shop on 97th and Jasper Ave. Again, he vanished!

I stayed with the coffee shop patrons who were ex-cons and sex-trade workers, talking about nothing important. I bummed drinks and felt right at home as the place began filling up with junkies and dealers, escaping from the stinging snowflakes shooting sideways in the powerful wind.

It was closing time and even the most violent street wise drunks and junkies, and ex-cons, had a destination, a home, a party – but I had nowhere to go. I had blown my money in Vancouver, for alcohol. Benny said he had enough for us to get a hotel room. But I could not find him, this so-called friend of mine.

How I made it through the blinding snow, other than survival mode, I will never know. That night I broke into a skid row type building, no, more of a foul smelling and freezing dump. The wind was too loud to hear me breaking in. I walked up creaky stairs to a bathroom where the wind was less. I laid my head against a plugged toilet and for fear of intruders, kept my foot pressed against the broken door.

As the howling blizzard slammed against the building, trying to get in, I felt cheap wine burning my gut. Somehow it was comforting to me.

Benny and I met the next day. He had stayed nice and warm in somebody's house. I don't remember who. We trudged through snow and ice to breakfast at the Salvation Army and that is when I suggested we get jobs at the Nickel Mine in Thompson, Manitoba. He turned his nose up at my suggestion but finally, accepted. We travelled by train, arrived, and stayed in the Single Men's Quarters. Benny worked Surface while I was in the Mine.

I came off shift one night to find that Benny had tried to kill himself with an overdose of pills. For him, the weather was too harsh, the work too hard, and he was homesick for Victoria. Far as I knew he had gone his own way. It was so cold, but I crossed from my quarters to the mess hall in a T shirt. The thermometer outside was way, way below zero! When I got back to the Single Men's Quarters, I wrote a letter to my girlfriend who lived in Edmonton.

Not long after at the Mine, I was about six hundred feet below ground, and walking in the drift (tunnel). I walked past a man who could hardly speak any English. At 3 pm, he was to stop any miners from walking past him. An explosion to break rock, had been set. Being half drunk, however, I walked into the area but did not know I was supposed to stop. I almost jumped out of my skin when "Kaboom!!!" I was not close enough to get hurt. But because I did not want to get the tunnel watcher 'the guard' in trouble, (he was new to Canada, and had a wife and family) I was fired by the Shift Boss.

Death Row inmates

I was thinking about my first night at the Needle Exchange and the years we had worked with street addicts, and others. One or two funerals I had attended came to mind. And I wondered if the message I had prepared from my bible was going to help anyone this night. Well, it had already helped me, so I thanked the Lord.

I said, "hello" to two or three clients and one asked me for a bible. She had considered the Needle Exchange through our Connection to Freedom meeting, to be her weekly "church". Another person "weekly spiritual lessons". Considering this place was the darkest spiritually, in the city of Victoria, I believed that God was making inroads.

A member of our group told me before our meeting how he was writing to Death Row inmates in Texas and California, and asked if I would like the addresses to write to them also. But I was already corresponding with inmates locally, across Canada, and with an inmate at the Corcoran State Prison in California, as well as speaking at schools. I just didn't see that I had the extra time to write more letters. But God has a way, and with Him, nothing is impossible.

While attending the Mustard Seed Street Church who also supported Connection to Freedom meetings and loaned us space, I heard a prison ministry team speak about their ministry to California prisoners. They encouraged we of the congregation to pray and if God moved us, to write to Death Row inmates at San Quentin. They themselves had worked with and were ministering to inmates at Chuckwalla as they lived in Blythe, California for six months and Victoria for the rest of the year. While listening to the speakers I was reminded of the Needle Exchange client and how he had asked me if I wanted the addresses to "Death Row inmates in Texas and California".

A month passed since I heard the testimony of the two speakers, and I had prayed regularly about making a connection with the Death Row inmates at San Quentin. But I was very busy with preparation for school speaking commitments, and bible counseling with newly released inmates of VIRCC, and William Head Institution, in the space loaned to me by Centennial United Church.

Suddenly it came to me! For my school talks I had used various props to support my topic. For example, letters from Needle Exchange clients about the consequences of drug abuse, and at another school I read a letter from a VIRCC inmate having a warning to students about the consequences of crime. "Why don't I ask a Death Row inmate in California to send me a letter with the consequences of crime?" This might help him as well!

So, I looked online and found the address and wrote a letter to Death Row, San Quentin. I shared my faith in Jesus Christ as the opening, and described my work with schools, and how it would be helpful to me and the classes, if he would write a letter about the consequences of making poor choices. I left the topic up to the inmate. As was common for me I asked for God's blessing on all that I had written. I posted the letter one night after a Connection to Freedom meeting. About two months later a package much bulkier than an envelope arrived from the United States. Immediately I saw "San Quentin" stamped on it. Because it was not a letter of response only, which I expected, I thought I had somebody's mail by mistake. But I carefully read every word and sure enough the package was for me! I became excited! When I opened the brown paper, I was amazed!

The inmate had written a warm letter that shared his faith, and he had drawn pictures on three sheets of white cardboard: The consequences of alcohol and drug abuse, the consequences of youth gangs, the consequences of bullying. The artwork was masterful!!! I shared the illustrations with The Mustard Seed Board of Directors, and with Lorne Chan, a schoolteacher, and friend, and a Camosun College Criminal Justice Program class. I wrote a letter of appreciation to the San Quentin inmate on Death Row and as I was scribing my letter prayerfully, I couldn't help but remember the Needle Exchange client who first spoke with me about his commitment to correspond with Death Row inmates in Texas and California.

I remembered a letter I had received from a Chaplain at the Texas Department of Corrections in Huntsville, Texas. Janet, my co-worker, and I had sent a copy of the Connection to Freedom book, and his response encouraged me to keep writing.

"Bail Supervisor's file"

I was remembering a blond woman from Louisiana who I took out for dinner when her and I were on passes from the psychiatric hospital. She was a teacher, I think. My thoughts of her vanished as a taxi pulled up to take me downtown. We passed a church on the way, and this got me thinking and remembering. After I received salvation through my Christian friend Ross, an old school buddy, the first time I read the bible I believed God was talking with me about my addictions: "See, I have taken out of your hand The cup of trembling... Isaiah 51:22. Nobody knew I was half stoned when I received my baptism a week later. I tried but I couldn't give up the heroin.

When I was dealing heroin just before I got busted and was put in prison, I had a solid girlfriend. So, because I was addicted to heroin myself, and so was she, I supported us both with my burglaries, and different crimes. The police raided us a few times but found nothing. I was caught at a downtown pawn shop with stolen goods. It was "chicken one day and feathers the next". A couple of years later my girlfriend left me. And I took a government sponsored alcohol and drug program as part of my bail supervision stipulations for another crime. I was told by an employment counselor "You're going to jail anyway, why worry about getting a job!"

I was scrounging around downtown looking to buy some Dilaudid. I was sick from needing them. The doctor gave me a script for 72 #4's. This was my third script. I was sitting at a table in a bar. There were two other guys, ex-cons I had done time with, sitting there. And a young woman about 20, sat down across from me. She asked if anybody was looking to score some dope. She had one or two Dilaudid as I remember. The next thing I knew, she and I were sitting at another bar. Then we took a motel room. Hard to believe that I was a Christian and I was awaiting trial for attempted robbery of a drug store. She had a bad record with the police as well.

At the motel we got high, and wanted more dope, so I drove us downtown but unfortunately, I was in an accident with a brick wall. Both of us were out on bail, so we ran up an alley, and got ourselves lost near a popular tavern. Because we didn't get caught, I thanked God, as near as I could anyway. She would soon visit me at the jail I would soon be sentenced to and would bring me some heroin.

Back at the motel I looked at a sign on the wall, motel rules, I guessed. Still feeling thankful, in a drugged-up sort of way, I took a bible from the desk. I knew one or two verses. But suddenly, I became very preachy as if I was some kind of bible teacher. My woman seemed impressed! So, I spewed more gibberish.

She fell asleep I guess from boredom. While she slept, and totally unaware that our relationship would last four years, I looked at what I had believed to be the Motel Rules. I stood there almost trembling as I read, "For God so loved the world that He gave His only begotten Son, that whoever believes in Him should not perish but have everlasting life." John 3:16. I felt this scripture touch me: spiritually, mentally, and in my flesh (my body). My Bail Supervisor, wrote my words down for his file, "I'm going back to Jesus!"

Pleurisy in prison

The weather was chilly. Still, there I was swinging a heavy sledgehammer into a wall by the Piggery. There was half a dozen of us in this work gang. I guess I was showing off because I was in pretty good physical shape from working construction.

The rest of the day went OK. I ate well, slept, but next morning when I went to make my bunk as I was reaching for a corner of the blanket, a sudden agonizing pain made me freeze. All I could do for the rest of the day was lie on my bunk and try not to move. By nighttime I had a raging fever and was falling in and out of consciousness.

The Medical Officer was called, and he tried taking my temperature from the dim light of the catwalk. Because it was close to Christmas, he had been drinking and as he staggered from one foot to the other, I could smell the booze on his breath. Moose, this friend of mine from the East Wing, called out: "If you don't get Steve some proper medical attention, we're going to riot!"

I didn't know if I was going to live or die, only that I felt like I had a fire inside of me. Sweat poured from me like drops of warm rain. Suddenly it seemed, it was morning and there were two unfamiliar guards in my cell, telling me, they were going to be taking me to the St. Joseph Hospital.

I felt very ill and confused and very hot in my jacket, that I wanted to rip off me. They handcuffed me and the next thing I remember is I'm sitting in the hospital intake area listening to the tapping of a typewriter. The intake nurse cautioned the guards not to leave me alone with her. She asked questions of one of the guards: "Inmate's name and number? Date of birth? What is the name of the jail where the inmate is from?"

The two guards couldn't agree on the name of the institution. One answered "Oakalla Prison Farm- Vancouver Island Unit". She typed it in her report. Eventually I was taken to my hospital room. The nurse nervously said, "You'll have to leave a guard outside the inmate's door. That's hospital procedure!"

It was the most miserable two weeks dealing with Pleurisy and feeling like a piece of garbage. However, the Jail doctor, who was looking after me, was lenient by allowing me to take a bath, instead of a shower for a couple of days back at the old jail Infirmary, so I didn't catch another cold, or worse.

It was Christmas Eve 1966 when, a guard who was Crown in rank, handed me a Christmas card and bag of candies called a 'Sunshine Package'. They were left for me by a volunteer with the Salvation Army. The card said, "Jesus loves you, Steve". I thought that funny, as did the guard.

The craziest meetings

One evening I had argued the reality of salvation with a man whose penchant for robbing banks was known well on the street. I suggested we take our argument outside, to which he angrily agreed. Although I realized this could mean a physical scuffle, or even worse, the peace of the Holy Spirit took over. I know this because I heard myself speaking in a loving manner as opposed to the violence, I was ready to use to protect myself.

I shared salvation with him, but he said, he was already "a Christian". Still, from that point on we met each other at Connection to Freedom meetings that were held at the Mustard Seed, and the Salvation Army Addiction Recovery Centre. I looked forward to seeing him at every meeting because we had become friendly with one another. That is, friendly in the Lord, on my part.

Probably the "craziest meeting" out of many years of facilitating the group, came one summer evening near 7pm. All day long I had felt uneasy in my spirit, although I had studied the scriptures and made preparation to reach out with my Bible message. It began when a woman of the street, obviously high on heroin, went to the bathroom. I felt a great uncertainty rip right through me! Then confusion took a strangle hold, and finally, I was filled with fear that the woman who went to the washroom, had overdosed!

How could I simply stand up and go and see how she was doing? Because a second woman, again, obviously high on heroin, ignoring the Connection to Freedom meeting had walked right into the washroom where the other woman had gone to the bathroom.

The first woman returned to her seat at the meeting but couldn't hold her head up. For a moment my mind went blank as if taking a break from insanity. A group member telephoned an ambulance. One attendant said to me, and remember this was before the Naloxone kits, "You called us just in time to save her life!" To see that woman on a stretcher at the Connection to Freedom meeting, I will never forget.

Visit to Prince George jail

I remembered how I had once shot pool with a man who had served time in Minnesota, Oklahoma, and the state of Washington, where, in a letter he told me of his need and desire to complete his high school education. We had corresponded with each other for quite some time. I shared my faith in God with him, and how my life was dramatically changed by Jesus when I was in the Vancouver Island Regional Correctional Centre, in 1987. I shared with him the Connection to Freedom meetings, and group book, and he said he thought that was a good idea if it helps people like him. I told him of the inmate I met when I was in the corrections camp, Lakeview Forestry Camp, who had served time in the state of Washington at the McNeil Island Federal Penitentiary. He told me of an inmate there who was a serial killer who played guitar. These were my thoughts in 1992.

Two members of Emmanuel Baptist Church who were supporting Connection to Freedom's meetings, financially, and spiritually through prayer, suggested I take a trip to meet with inmates in Prince George. At the time I was working with a Matsqui Institution inmate who had just been paroled. He was a Christian who had spent many years behind bars for bank robbery. I asked his parole officer for permission to take him with me to Prince George. He gave the OK.

We left Victoria in the middle of winter by car, him driving, but the further away we got the colder it became. The Ferry trip to Vancouver, followed by one or two stops for meals, and then after we had travelled four- or five-hours snow accompanied us. Miles of white was all we could see. I remembered how from Prince George, a Chaplain was to meet us, and take us around the provincial jail there.

When we pulled into Prince George the temperature was frigid and the snow was falling sideways, in a bitterly cold wind. The Chaplain who knew our Emmanuel Baptist Church supporters, had a great sense of humor. The first thing he did was lock me and my co-worker, the Matsqui parolee, behind bars. Before anxiety could set in, however, the Chaplain unlocked the door, and with a smile, welcomed us to Prince George jail, which we were to find out, the inmates called "The Hill".

We had arrived near lunch time, so the Chaplain took us almost next door to a Coffee Shop. There we would see, once again, his sense of humor. The waitress asked, "Have you made a decision?" Smiling the Chaplain replied, "Yes, a decision for Jesus Christ. How about you?" The waitress, the parolee, my co-worker, and I, laughed!

The Chaplain we were to find out also pastored a very large church. We talked about that for a while, and then we were given free rein to walk around the jail. It was suggested we visit every cell to introduce ourselves and ask if we could be of any help.

Some of the cells had makeshift toilets, and in fact the jail was in poor shape. The inmates were young, middle aged, and one or two were older men. We asked, "May we pray for you or help any other way?" Some requested prayer, and one inmate, an older man, asked for prayers for his family matters. I prayed with him and he asked about Connection to Freedom meetings. After some hours the Chaplain asked if we were staying in Prince George, but we kindly declined, because of the weather. He prayed for "travelling mercies" for us.

"Writing My Story" Exercise

Try not to write about anything to do with the criminal justice system. Instead, think about a time in your life when you experienced happiness, not with drugs or alcohol, but before all that. Did you ever have an interest in sports, fishing, or writing? Perhaps your favourite pet, or a vehicle you enjoyed? How about God or church? Or chapel? Unless a group leader or facilitator is leading this exercise, you can take all the time you want to write your story. If you want to you can sign one initial of your first name, and the date. But you don't have to if you don't choose to.

My Story

_____

_____

_____

_____

_____

_____

_____

_____

_____

_____

_____

_____

_____

_____

_____

_____

_____

_____

_____

_____

Date: _____ Initial _____

Letter from Argentina

Alberto, whose testimony you are about to read, has been a friend of mine for many years. We have remained in contact to 2021, by social media, and longer. He is from Milano, Italy, and came to our "Connection to Freedom" meetings, not as an addict or ex-offender but because 'an addict' he was reaching out to had died a drug-related death. The man who died had attended our meetings on several occasions. At that time, our group met at the Needle Exchange on Commercial Alley. God has guided Alberto through thick and thin since he left our meetings. So here now, as written from Buenos Aires, Argentina, is an excerpt from Alberto's letter.

"My experience in Argentina is getting more exciting because now I'm serving the Lord as a missionary, photographer, and writer. I want you and the 'Connection to Freedom' group to see what I have been up to these last seven months.

"After starting in April, I finished my journalism course at the end of June. Then in July and August we went to Paraguay where I met an ancient tribe called 'the Ache'. I am also sending along an informative newsletter which includes my articles and photos about how God is using me in this part of the world.

"I have seen God reflected in the huge community that lives in the Triple Frontier. Certainly, the Lord has been revealing to me gifts and skills that I have but wouldn't have recognized them without His help. Still some traits of my own character like pride and rebellion remain evident to me and I need to work on them.

"God is guiding me step by step to develop the good qualities in me and to recognize my 'enemies' and the need to sometimes wage spiritual 'warfare'. I need to work more on the Holy Spirit that I got when I was saved in Mexico. It's now been two and a half years since I was saved. I miss you 'Connection to Freedom' members and I hope the Lord will allow me to be in Victoria again. Perhaps in March, God willing. I will check your website again, Steve. Take care, group, and much love always."

Alberto.

Note: If you look at the front of this book you will see two pictures of the author. They were both taken by Alberto, who won an award for his "Street Stories" photography.

Letter to a California inmate

I shared this, my testimony, in a letter to a California inmate.

I have never forgotten the elderly Black people who said, "Hey mister, please help us! Our house is burning!" Donny, my Kentucky friend, and I looked through the coffee shop window that faced the shanty huts of the black section of Victorville. Smoke billowed from an E Street dwelling. Donny and I jumped up together! He called out to me: "Let's help them, Steve!" "Hey man, I'm right with you!" I answered. Then I felt a rush of adrenaline. The Black people thanked us as their eyes filled with tears over fear for their families. I can't say for sure that I would have done it on my own. But, side by side, Donny and I ran across the tracks onto E Street toward the fire.

There was a crowd of Black men and women gathered, as amazed at seeing two white men running toward them as they were shocked by the fire. I admit I was drunk, and my friend was feeling no pain. The scene seemed surreal with the stench of smoke and burned wires. We pulled an old hose and sprayed water while a fire truck, probably from the 1940's era, chugged along the street ringing a single lonely bell. Covered in soot, Donny and I returned home after providing whatever help we could. I've got to be honest: I felt like a hero. I never did find out if the fire was the result of racial hatred or an overloaded electrical circuit. My buddy, looking like a coal miner, called out: "See 'yawl' in the morning, Steve!" "OK, Donny," I replied.

The following morning at work I could not understand why Donny, my friend and fellow 'hero,' avoided me. It made me feel very uncomfortable. As if he were a child who had been threatened by an angry parent for disobedience, his face showed fear. I didn't have to wait long to find out the reason for my friend's timidity. Donny had been mocked by fellow workmates led by Vince, the biggest racist. He hated me for helping the Black family. Scornfully, Vince said, "Steve, I guess you like them kind of people, don't you, boy? I was just starting to take a liking to you but you, helping those Black people last night, sure stopped that. You're just a punk, kid! If you don't get careful, we'll take you out back and bury you in the desert!" Vince had spit racist hatred at me like a snake spits poison. I felt embarrassed, ashamed, confused, and terrified. Our job supervisor, it seemed, was unavailable. I was all alone.

Days later there was a blinding, biting sandstorm. The windows and doors of my motel room were being pelted by sand that blocked out the sun, causing complete darkness until the blowing subsided. It was as if a message for me was in the wind, and I shouldn't miss it. The news, it turned out, was in my mailbox in the form of a note. I was surprised to read an invitation for lunch from a young Black couple, George, and Mavis. When I decided to accept, I was perfectly aware that I might take a beating or even be killed by racists who would become aware of me accepting the lunch invitation. This threat was very real to me.

I arrived at the run-down shack on E Street and was amazed to see a big pink Cadillac parked outside. The car, it turned out, had no motor, and was fit for only junk. I was greeted with a smile by Mavis and then shocked to find myself walking on a floor made of dirt. On an old stove, Mavis was boiling greens in a large saucepan. I ate with my hosts as they laughed at my dislike for greens. To my surprise, not one word was said to me at work. This was a relief I did not expect. However, the supervisor called me to his office and said he was transferring me to Los Gatos, miles away, toward San Fransisco. I didn't know how to feel, except loneliness set in at the thought of being so far away from my Victorville friends, especially my Mexican girlfriend, 18 like me, who I loved, and had planned to marry. But I was to find out, I had sabotaged this possibility with my drinking.

Two weeks later in Los Gatos on the job I met two older men from Missouri, both heavy racists but I didn't find out until we had moved in together. They say one alcoholic can spot another a mile away. We rented a house together on Broadway Street. But with the beach at Santa Cruz close and San Jose even closer, I knew where I was going to be spending my time on weekends. I was very appreciative of my Minnesota co-worker who had helped me with the money to buy my car, a grey 1955 Mercury Montclair with a continental kit on the back.

One night at a hamburger stand in San Jose, I met a woman younger than my 18 years. Of course I was drunk at the time. After two months she gave me an alternative for my drinking. She lost! But truthfully, I was falling apart for my Mexican girlfriend in Victorville. We had planned to move to Canada, and she, being a hairdresser, in Carmel, was willing to work as a hairdresser in Saanich. I hated myself for not being able to stop my drinking.

After work one early evening I drove to Santa Cruz, but almost hit a traffic cop with my right fender. Returning to Los Gatos, drunk, I thought police sirens behind me were cats that had somehow jumped onto my car's back seat and were meowing. Re-entering Los Gatos, and my Broadway Street driveway, the police surrounded me and questioned me: "Where are you from?" I replied, "Paris, Illinois!" "Where do you live?" "Right here!" "Have you been drinking?" "Maybe, one or two beers" I slurred. "Were you trying to kill yourself?" one cop asked. Saying "No," I lied to him. "We're taking your car!" Then he said I could get it from the impound lot after I paid the fines.

Having been fired because of my drunken antics giving a bad name on the company I worked for, no money, because of my addiction to alcohol, considering whether to steal a car, the next morning early, with a pounding head, and bloodshot eyes, I caught a ride with a trucker. He was headed to an area near the Greater Mojave Desert town of Trona, then on to his home in Los Angeles, as memory serves me. This was hundreds of miles from Los Gatos.

In this small desert town where I worked as employee for a housing project, racist attitudes were rampant. So, much so, that only when I drank, including with my boss, could I escape the bigotry. This was my experience as a youth in California.

But did I use the bigotry of others, as an excuse to drink? Let me answer this way. Decades since I had a meal with George and Mavis, the African American couple in Victorville, I have never had a meal, whether celebration dinner, or any, that was as special to me, as their lunch of greens, when I was 18 years old. Besides that, never have I met a woman, who I loved as much as my Latino girlfriend. By God's grace, daily, I am sober.

The California inmate at Kern Valley State Prison who read this, my testimony, replied with his own experiences of "racism" and addiction recovery. We shared our lives with each other, and 2013, was his last letter. Often, I feel myself praying for him.

Letter from a VIRCC inmate

GM had attended a Chapel service where the Chaplain was handing out copies of my story in 'The Bakersfield Californian' newspaper. Because he had lived in California's High Desert, the inmate felt a connection to me, so he said in his letter. Prayerfully, I sought God's will, and I felt confident and therefore I provided support to my "California friend." Here are excerpts from GM's story. I am on probation, living in a recovery house in Victoria, British Columbia, Canada. I had been at Vancouver Island Regional Correctional Centre. I am giving my story to Steve of the 'Connection to Freedom' group in hope of getting my message out to young people about the abuse of steroids and the consequences that I had lived with every day of my life.

Just then, I, Steve, remembered a time in my life: A member of our Connection to Freedom addict and ex-offender support group, Terry, (not his real name) killed a drug dealer and was charged with manslaughter. But they couldn't find him, so police officers came to my home and picked me up and took me downtown for questioning. Under my breath I cursed Terry. I had given him money for his rent, and after he spent it on drugs, I had visited him at Detox. Now this is the thanks I get! As if they suspected I had killed the heroin addict, I was interrogated by the police! One cop, frustrated by not getting any answers said to me, "There's a man that isn't breathing anymore, and somebody is going to pay for it!" (I suppose, if I didn't give them information about Terry's whereabouts, it could just as easily have been me who was going to be charged with murder!) Charged with murder! Me? There were many bad memories that came to mind that night at the Police Station.

Like when I was hauled in and my head smashed against the iron bunk in the cells. I thought back to when, sick from heroin withdrawal, a policeman questioned me for hours about a Credit Union that had been robbed. I was ghastly ill, unable to think and almost admitted to the crime just to get some peace. He asked me "how would you like a fix? Nobody will have to know. You know how the game is played; tell me who robbed the Credit Union. It was you, wasn't it?" These thoughts were parading through my mind like drunken sailors. Never have I wanted to leave a place so badly in my life. But it was 1990 now and my life had changed when I was in jail. I had started the support group and was a benefit to the community, so I thought.

But I hadn't forgotten the cop who had smashed my foot in his car door or the ones who laughed at me when I tried to press charges, standing there on crutches. Being handcuffed in the back of a police wagon, while a cop doubled me over with his fists, wasn't very funny either. But the worst thing to come to mind was 1986 when both my lady and I were out on bail. These two well-known undercover officers; one who was to testify at my trial, had told my cousin, "Steve and the woman he lives with, should be wrapped in a rug and thrown in the river. They are no good. The world would be better off without both!"

There was a horrible satisfaction that came when I remembered how I had tried to stab a cop, with the jagged end of a broken wine bottle, before I was hit from behind and knocked out cold. Welcome three months in the Psych Ward. I've got to get out of here- this Police Station is a nightmare! Should I call a lawyer I wonder? For what, I haven't done anything! These are just bad memories and vibes from being here. Wow, if a youth at risk could see inside my head, he'd never commit a crime. Remembering how Christ saved me, I forgave the police. (Mark 11:25-26)

As I walked away from the Victoria Police Station a thought crossed my mind: "This is what you do, Steve. Don't think it strange! You are defending your support group member with the little information you have." I stood up for Terry in Court and supported him while he was at William Head Institution for four years, and at his Parole Hearing. I had given him help that seemed unappreciated on his part. I should have learned by now. Surprise! I received a telephone call from Terry, who was working in another province, and he thanked me on behalf of himself and his family, for the Connection to Freedom meetings.

But that was the past, and I know I have been forgiven.

GM telephoned me late one night to ask if I would marry him and his girlfriend. Their choice for the wedding was the Breakwater so they could take photos. But before the groom and his bride, and their guests could congregate for the happy affair, a howling wind, blasted and pounded us. The ocean waves splashed! Hats flew off heads and skirts blew! Papers scattered! But, holding on to my Bible as pages flicked back and forth, I read: And now abide faith, hope, love, these three; but the greatest of these is love. 1 Corinthians 13:13

Next is the newspaper article that the Chaplain of the Vancouver Island Regional Correctional Centre handed out to inmates.

Bakersfield Californian newspaper

Finding Salvation on a Lonely Desert Highway

Steve Bradley knows what it's like to lie down in the middle of a bleak desert highway, stars vivid overhead in the clear, pitch-black sky, the whistle of a car in the distance, speeding ever closer.

He knows what it's like to be at peace with the inevitability of asphalt, metal and flesh coming together in one violent, last embrace.

He knows because he lived it one night in the Kern County desert exactly 40 years ago.

He's shared the tale dozens of times, perhaps hundreds. He calls it his "California story," and if he forgets to share it when he speaks to students or inmates or addicts, someone who's heard it before will invariably ask him to tell it again for the others' benefit.

So Bradley will tell them about that night on Inyokern Road, about the hollowness of utter despair, about discovering hope where none could possibly have survived.

It starts at dusk on July 4, 1965.

Bradley had been drinking beer all day at the Bonanza, a bar in the desolate desert town of Trona.

He'd been thinking about his father, the man he looked to for everything, who'd died of leukemia two years earlier back in Victoria, British Columbia.

He'd been thinking about how, since he left home, he'd lost a car, an apartment, a girlfriend, and any semblance of will or ambition. And hitchhiking to Trona two months earlier, at the end of an aimless trek through California, hadn't changed things.

He was working as a handyman for a construction company, building homes for employees of a local mining company. He'd been sleeping wherever he could find a place to curl up. "The nights were cold," he said, "but I was always drunk."

It was no way to live and, at 18, he decided there was no sense in bothering to continue.

So he slugged down his last beer, walked out the door and stuck out his thumb. He got as far as a gas station two miles west of Inyokern.

"I had a comb on me, half a pack of Winston cigarettes and nine pennies. It was 10 cents for a bottle of Coke back then and I asked the guy at the gas station if he could help me with the 10th cent. He said, 'Sorry, can't.'"

The last straw! Bradley walked a little way farther up the highway and stopped. He was done. Done walking, done caring, done living. "I lay down in the middle of the road," Bradley said. "I was actually excited. The only joy I had was that it would soon be over."

The car took a long time, but it came. He remembers feeling his own warm blood. Then, at some point during the night, he heard a car stop, then footsteps and the sense that someone was standing over him.

"I wanted to scream, 'I've changed my mind! Can you help me?' But they ran away, jumped in their car, and screamed out of there," Bradley said.

The headline in the following afternoon's Californian got the essentials right: "Hitchhiker, hit-run victim, near death." Bradley had been discovered along the side of the road by a couple of China Lake sailors returning to their base from Bakersfield.

He'd been whisked to a hospital in Ridgecrest, where he told California Highway Patrol Officer Ralph Johnson that he'd been hit while hitchhiking. He didn't mention suicide. Fearful that he'd be arrested for underage drinking, he told Johnson he was 21.

He had bigger problems: a broken pelvis, a fractured right ankle, and intestinal injuries. Doctors didn't expect him to survive, according to the article.

But he'd been wearing a heavy jacket that his father had given him, a bulky coat with thick leather buttons. When the car hit him -- Nevada plates, by one witness account -- Bradley had been spun onto his belly and drug along the road. Those thick buttons were shaved down to the thickness of copper pennies. Bradley likes to think they were just thick enough to save his life.

Of course, there was also Dr. Robert Hamblin, who kept him alive on the operating table the next morning. Bradley stayed several weeks at the Ridgecrest hospital – long enough to celebrate his 19th birthday – and was then transported to Kern General Hospital in Bakersfield. After several more weeks, he was returned to British Columbia via air ambulance.

The imagined Hallmark Hall of Fame version of Bradley's story has him emerging from weeks of physical therapy a new man – physically, emotionally, and spiritually healed. The fact is, though, his injuries lingered. He was forced to wear a colostomy bag and endured epileptic seizures for 22 years. Worse, though, he became addicted to alcohol and heroin.

In 1986, strung out, he attempted to rob a drug store. He was caught, convicted, and incarcerated for 18 months – and, in his cell, again contemplated suicide. Instead, he changed.

"At 41 years old, I realized I'd hit rock bottom," he said. "I knew that either I was going to kill myself or I was going to give myself to God."

In 1987 he founded a Victoria-based program that pushes heroin addicts, alcoholics, and others toward recovery. He lectures, runs therapy sessions, and works with the city's needle exchange program. He created a well-regarded addiction workbook.

It took an extra 22 years, but the lesson of Inyokern Road finally took.

At 58, Bradley is lecturing less, having turned over more of the "street" program to younger staff members. But he still thinks about those two sailors, whose identity he never learned. He still thinks about that CHP officer.

And he still thinks about Inyokern Road.

"One day I'll have to go back and make peace with that patch of highway," he said. "Get closure. But then I feel closure every time I tell the story."

My thanks to Robert Price (now with KGET-17 TV) for permission to use his article from The Bakersfield Californian.

"Michael's view"

I have been an actor and filmmaker for quite a few years and have had my films screened across North America and the UK, and I feel Steve's life story could and hopefully one day will, be made into a movie. In fact, Steve has started working on a film outline for a possible future script.

Steve is a prolific writer and not only wrote his life story but recorded it on tape for me to listen to. I met Steve Bradley, leader of an addict, offender, and ex-offender support group in 2013. He had been leading this group and helping recovering addicts, offenders, and ex-offenders for more than twenty-five years.

Steve would also invite me to accompany him, in 2015, as a guest speaker at a local high school. He had dedicated many years to helping school students by telling his story.

Through his writing, Steve realized he was an actor. Until his healing to speak his emotions openly, Steve hid behind the masks of each character that he created for each phase of his life.

A recovering addict himself, Steve was a chameleon able to change his character to suit his surroundings whenever needed. There are a lot of honest reflections in his writing.

As professional actors, we in 'the business' can easily get caught up in the world of Hollywood, and its excesses. Acting is a difficult occupation, and we need to have very thick skin.

Thank you, Steve, for all you have done throughout your own journey, and for reaching out to those in the acting and filmmaking business.

Michael Farrell

March 14, 2023

"The Cold, Hard, Truth"

Keep in mind that youth at risk were the target of his story, as well as adults in prisons and the community. Here is GRD's story:

When I was on the street, I took OxyContin because it was available all over the place. I also became addicted to Dilaudid for a year. At the same time, I was still doing my crack! The one time I stopped using crack was when a doctor friend gave me some ecstasy from Switzerland. It cost me thirty dollars for 125 milligrams. This wasn't a street drug; it was what psychiatrists used for therapy over there. I was addicted for a year.

Then I switched back to cocaine. I used crack cocaine for sixteen years off and on, but mostly on. I didn't jump right into it. Instead, it was a series of events that led to my love for this horrendous drug. I can take alcohol or leave it alone, but crack has a hold on me that is overpowering. This is not your parents or teachers holding this information over your head; this is the cold, hard, truth!

You probably think blah, blah, blah, whatever, but if you're messing with coke, especially the rock, right now, I feel sorry for you. Sex or drugs won't cut it when you find yourself in a psychiatric institution for cocaine psychosis! I know because I've been there!

I have been told I look better today than I have for years. It feels wonderful to hear this. Thank you to those people kind enough to care. I have not always been an addict, active in my addictions and of no use to society. For instance, I have been a co-speaker at Camosun College with Chaplain Steve. That's when I pulled out my pocket-sized bible to tell the students about my faith in God.

I once held a private pilot's license and flew Cessna-150 planes in Sidney, BC. In Hawaii, I piloted a Cessna-150 up and into Haleakala Crater at the top of Maui. Also, I scuba-dived and swam with the giant sea turtles and reef sharks.

When I was going to Connection to Freedom groups in 2001 at the Needle Exchange, I was happy to donate a typewriter which was used to set up the Connection to Freedom Jail and Street Outreach Society.

One thing I would like to add is that dealers are putting fentanyl into cocaine, so beware!

It had always been my hope to go to college and train as a naturopath. So much for my dreams! I would like to say that I love the Lord and throughout my life, I have read the bible, which has given me my strength for recovery.

GRD,

Republished Easter 2024

Healing from "Grief!"

There is a purpose for me telling my story. I want to address the pain of grief, and hopefully, you will be helped should you too be suffering from grief. As a child I was taught by my dad to never show my feelings, to never cry, and to just get on with it. When we lost our first Connection to Freedom member from opioids mixed with sleeping pills, in 1987, I showed no emotions believing it would be best for the group, if I just got on with it. But deep grief was born in me that day. I hid behind my phony smiles and jokes, to avoid the pain of losing my friend, a group member.

Twenty-two years later seventeen members of Connection to Freedom meetings had died in their addictions to alcohol and/ or drugs. However, also in 2010, a group member overdosed on pills and alcohol. To hide my pain of overwhelming grief, thinking it best for the group I never cried. Although I was sick with grief, I never showed my true feelings, and as my dad's teachings in my childhood, had taught me, I never cried. I just got on with it. I pulled up my bootstraps. But, in my core that makes me human, because of these deaths, I felt like a dismal failure. "Why them and why not me?" I began blaming myself. My grief was killing me, and I was ready to go. The last death was a young man who played his guitar at the group and sang very uplifting songs that he had written. He had committed suicide and was found by the Delta Police. The young man's family assured me that he had a mental illness that was unrecognizable unless you were a doctor suited to such a case. I continued blaming myself questioning "Why them and why not me?"

As the deceased group members began to haunt my dreams, I felt myself tumbling towards a nervous breakdown! It was then from out of the blue I received a telephone call from a woman who had attended our Connection to Freedom meetings for years and had realized the meetings saved her life. She served on our board of directors. She also became a credentialled social worker, after attending Camosun College, and University of Victoria courses. The reason for her phone call was to let me know about a six -week program, called 'Grief, Loss, and Life Transitions'. You might say that I received this information in the nick of time! Because

I was on the edge of a nervous breakdown. So, I attended the program, still feeling jittery, and unsure of myself.

As a Christian first then Chaplain, in a class of about twelve, I shared Jesus Christ as my hope. I was very thankful that my friend and sometime Connection to Freedom meeting facilitator, Kurt, had joined the class also. I'm so grateful for what I learned which included forgiveness for my dad for his teaching me to never show my emotions, to never shed a tear.

Those six weeks of digging into my grief, discussing my losses, including those in my Connection to Freedom meeting who had died, I felt that a huge weight was lifting from me, a small piece at a time. At the end of the last session, we each received a certificate. Mine said 'Certificate of Completion to Chaplain Steve Bradley'. Because the piece of paper was so important to me (I had learned to forgive my dad) I placed it in a frame and hung it on the wall at home.

Whenever I feel the need to remember, I think of my first talk at Camosun College accompanied by Bev, my co-worker with Connection to Freedom meetings, and program co-facilitator at the Vancouver Island Regional Correctional Centre. She said,

"I have known Steve Bradley for 18 months and worked with him at the prison. I also helped him with the support group that he holds at Mustard Seed. And Steve, please don't be offended by what I am about to say, but I'm trying to help the students understand how hard it is for people with addictions, that come out of jail, to no support". She glanced at me, and I nodded as if I was in control. She continued, "I have worked with Steve in all kinds of situations and watched him help others, often in crisis. In all this time, I have never seen him show any emotions. He is like a robot. Honestly, working with Steve is like working with a robot. Sorry, Steve, I just needed to let the students know how hard it is for people like you, if they don't have any support." -Bev.

Grief is a terrible feeling and can cripple emotionally unless you look after yourself. If you are in prison, and you have access to my workbook, I encourage you to try the exercises, and to give serious consideration to giving your life to Jesus Christ. He is the One who gave me healing from grief.

Two years later I ran into a former Connection to Freedom member, who told me of his sobriety. Unfortunately, a month or so after our meeting, he died of heroin laced with fentanyl. I counted the eighteenth death of people who had died from their addictions. But I didn't grieve as such but felt a certain sadness. I do not consider those eighteen whose lives were taken mostly by their own choices. I knew that I had shared Jesus Christ with each one and encouraged them through God's word. I will always remember how my dear friend who is a social worker, reached out to me and thereby saved my life, by telling me about the program: Grief, Loss, and Life Transitions. Thank you, Sis!

It is 2024 and I no longer feel the grief due to the loss of eighteen group members. I am convinced that each one is in a much better place than the world has to offer. If you are grieving for whatever reason, *"Draw near to God and He will draw near to you." James 4:8*

Reima-Lee's Story

Sadly, I update my testimony to October 6, 2022. I was to meet with a relative of mine who is a troubled youth. Before we could get together, he was murdered. Youth gangs and drugs were the cause.

From my mom's side, I am from the Soda Creek First Nations Band located in Williams Lake, B.C. She has had a lot of struggles in her life from the abuse that residential schools inflicted on her and many other First Nations people. My dad was German and served in the American military. His name was Gary and he resided in California. But he was drafted to fight in Vietnam and never made it back from that war. This is my testimony:

From kindergarten to when I was in grade school I was bullied until I rebelled by fighting back when I was fifteen. I was a high school dropout and I left home when I was just sixteen years old. It wasn't my biological family and, quite honestly, I wasn't considered part of their family. Shortly thereafter, I was invited to live in a foster home. By the time I turned seventeen, I was already addicted to alcohol and cigarettes. I also used acid, mushrooms, pills, and cocaine, and I smoked pot, but it was ecstasy that would become my greatest downfall.

I worked as a housekeeper at hotels off and on over the years before ending up on welfare as my addictions grew worse. At age twenty I became pregnant and had my son. His dad and I were married for several years. Our marriage ended in 1998, mostly due to alcohol abuse by both of us. Then a few months later I nearly died from a phony ecstasy pill sold to me at a rave in Vancouver. I was the victim of an evil trick. This was just like the phony pills with fentanyl in them these days that have caused so many overdose deaths. I later learned it had been PCP that had almost killed me.

It was an eerie feeling, knowing I was dying, but there was nothing I could do about it. Luckily, someone found me and instructed me not to fall asleep. I fought for my life, but only when I visualized my six-year-old son being left without his mom. Otherwise, I couldn't have cared less.

But I kept going. Shortly after that, I lost my son to the B.C. government's family and children's ministry. My life had been turned upside down and couldn't get much worse, I thought, but I was dead wrong. That same year I fell into a drug-induced psychosis from taking too much ecstasy, acid, pot, and alcohol. As a result, I ended up being arrested and committed to a psych ward.

Months later, when I was released, I attended drug and alcohol programs, including NA and AA, to help get my life back on track. Then I attended a couple of residential treatment centres on the mainland, including a recovery house. I had even ventured down to Commercial Alley in Victoria one night when I was feeling down and found the Connection to Freedom group having a meeting. They had borrowed space from The Needle Exchange.

It was my first introduction to a bible-based support group for addictions, and I remember how kind they were when they handed out sandwiches made and donated by a woman named Jane. They asked if they could say a prayer for me. I agreed, not thinking much about it. I left Victoria only to be reunited with the group a couple of years later. I moved to Kamloops around 2001 but was quickly arrested again, this time for stealing hundreds of dollars from a bar. I had left to play pool at another bar but by that time the police had been called and I was arrested. Back at the city cells, one of the police officers nearly broke my neck for my crime and I had to wear a neck brace. However, the bar owner didn't want to press charges and my neck injury likely contributed to my being released the next day. But this only fueled my addictions because the doctor in Kamloops prescribed me lots of Percocet and other opioid painkillers, including Dilaudid.

It was then I decided to move back to Victoria. However, I couldn't seem to avoid trouble. Once back I soon found myself in another cold jail cell, this time for fighting. Thankfully a women's group helped me out and that's when I ended up living at a women's shelter. I felt alone and destitute and didn't want to spend another cold, dark night sleeping on a park bench. I was still at the shelter when one night I pulled a book from the shelf to read. It was entitled "What Would Jesus Do?"

I had become a lost and bitter person, angry at the world, hating the people who had done me wrong. I had hit rock bottom a lot of times during my addictions and pretty much had seen it all: the deaths of other drug users, my own near-death experience and skid row and jail. At the shelter one night I had to walk over the dead body of a drug user I had been chatting with only hours earlier. Life wasn't good. I'd spent fifteen years immersed in my addictions. I had lost everything and was depressed. I had even contemplated suicide at times.

I missed my son and I wanted to change my life, but I couldn't. I didn't know how. So, getting back to being in the shelter in 2002 and looking down at the book in front of me, "What Would Jesus Do?" I prayed a heartfelt prayer for help, asking Jesus into my heart. I wasn't a praying person but that night I said a prayer.

When I went outside the house, perhaps a day or two later, a random stranger whom I never saw again handed me a business card. He told me about the Connection to Freedom meetings being held at The Needle Exchange. It was not far from the shelter, so I went to one of their meetings.

The Connection to Freedom people were happy and the one running the group was Steve. I then remembered our brief encounter years ago. He told me the word of God could change my life, and because Steve was an ex-heroin addict, I listened. He said I needed to forgive the people I hated if I wanted to come off drugs and alcohol. I was invited to come back the following week. That night in my spirit I heard, "You don't need to do drugs anymore." I believe this was God speaking to me because I dumped all my drugs and cigarettes into the toilet. This I know was my first step toward getting clean and sober.

It wasn't easy after that because I became sick for weeks from withdrawal. But I persevered because I wanted so desperately to be sober. I was in major pain, but I didn't go to a doctor because the Lord was helping me. I clung to my bible, praying through the worst of my withdrawals. My pain and sickness eventually subsided.

I believe God used the Connection to Freedom meeting to save my life. I haven't used drugs since 2002. I also quit smoking cigarettes and using alcohol for five years. A scripture verse that I got from a meeting helped me out:

"No temptation has overtaken you except such as is common to man but God is faithful who will not allow you to be tempted beyond what you are able but will make a way of escape that you may be able to bear it." (1 Corinthians 10:13).

I found a nice apartment to rent and spent time studying the word of God. Getting back to the present,

I applied for funding from the Soda Creek Band in 2003 to return to school, upgrade my studies and go to college. I was accepted and hit the books 100 percent "clean and sober" and "smoke free". For years I didn't even take so much as an over-the-counter pill for headaches. Getting completely clean was my mission and goal. I thank Jesus Christ; I was saved by grace.

I kept going to Connection to Freedom meetings, and I was asked to be the secretary for the Connection to Freedom Jail and Street Outreach Society sometime in 2004. I was on the board for seven years and, since I was still working on the problem of not being able to forgive, I went to bible counselling sessions with Steve who had become a chaplain. He had borrowed a room from the Centennial United Church for his counselling.

I worked on learning the word of God and studying for school. I also worked on mending my broken relationship with my son whom I had visited only off and on for several years because that's all I had been permitted.

But as I recovered and learned the ways of God, my son graduated from high school, worked at a job, and took some military training.

In 2008, I graduated from the University of Victoria in the school of social work with a BSW. In 2014 I graduated with an MSW specializing in indigenous studies.

One thing about Steve Bradley, who was our executive director, was that he never told anybody how he was feeling. In 2010 he almost had a nervous breakdown, and this was when I was glad, I had received my degrees so that I could help him. Steve had been grieving the loss of seventeen Connection to Freedom members. From the start of the group in 1987 he had watched the hand of death take seventeen of his friends. He blamed himself for each loss, asking, "Why them and not me?"

The same day he felt he was going to have a breakdown, in my spirit I heard, "Tell Steve." I never knew that Steve, our group leader, was in so much pain. He didn't let it show. But God saw his pain, and through Him, I sent an e-mail to Steve about a program of grief healing. I did this as a friend first and a social worker second. Steve attended the program, which was at the South Island Training Centre. It was entitled "Grief, Loss, and Life Transitions."

In 2021, with his bible as well, Steve is still working this program into his daily life and has learned to forgive himself. He says the e-mail I sent saved his life.

Today Steve says this about the group members who died from their addictions: "I do not grieve for the members we lost because God's word describes a far better place where they now live eternally."

My biological sister Melissa (AKA Missy) was twenty-five years old when she died in 2006 from suicide. Really it was from depression and the terrible things that had happened to her that caused her to end her life. She had never been addicted to anything in her life. This was extremely hard to accept, but I understood the depths of despair that one can go through struggling in life.

Warnings about drugs and the changes in my life were topics I spoke about to high school students with Steve. The talks, which began in 1992, ended in 2015, a year after Steve's retirement. I spoke to some youths at Parkland Secondary School five times warning them about making bad choices and about the consequences of using alcohol and drugs. Although there were a great many things that happened during my addictions, I've highlighted a few in the hope that someone who is struggling with their addictions knows there is hope. You must not give up, because Jesus loves you and has positive plans for your life. If you are willing to believe, your faith can move the mountains in your life.

"For I know the thoughts that I think toward you, says the LORD, thoughts of peace and not of evil, to give you a future and a hope. Then you will call upon Me and go and pray to Me, and I will listen to you. And you will seek Me and find Me when you search for Me with all your heart" (Jeremiah 29:11–14).

Reima-Lee
Re-posted March 27, 2024

My First Nations Friends

I recall a certain group at the Connection to Freedom meeting in 1991. We were a parolee of William Head Institution, a parolee of Kent Institution, and two others, both addicts and me, group facilitator. That morning with a study of God's word, I felt challenged by the question, "What is love?" That evening, I posed the question to the group: "What is love?" Across from me at the table were blank faces. I had no idea either. I felt more sadness than I had for years when I realized I could not answer the question because, and I'm ashamed to admit it, as with my group members, I had never allowed myself to feel love.

The justification was a proud, "I don't deserve it!" I had always acted my feelings, not experiencing them as true emotions. Love, I had always steered away from it, and if it got too close, I would always sabotage that relationship. This is common behavior for an addict because it always provides an excuse "to use." Since that Connection to Freedom meeting of 1991 or so, in my mind, I revisited that question: "Love … what is it?" Is it compassion for fellow humans? Comfort provided to a lonely senior by a friendly dog? Perhaps love for you is the smile of a baby that touches the hearts of brand-new parents? There is the love of one addict for another. Allow me to share the following personal experience:

I left Victoria, BC, to make a geographical change, because I thought with this move I could "break" my heroin addiction. I took a job working at an Alberta coal mine in Grande Cache and was sharing a trailer with my brother, a long-time coal miner, and his family. I had tried to con the company doctor out of narcotics, but he refused me, so I left for Edmonton to try and score some heroin. I spent whatever money I had on taxis, so I had to hitchhike back.

A wild and windy excursion back to Grande Cache saw me trapped in a blizzard. I'd been walking for hours it seemed; I was frozen to the bone. Fear then penetrated every fiber of my being when I heard the howl of what I believed was a wild animal. The countryside was bleak, unforgiving, and the temperature was bitterly cold to my face and hands. It may sound dramatic, but in my mind, I was going to die. Of course, what appeared to be hours standing beside the road was probably closer to half an hour. Nonetheless, I was afraid of freezing to death and the animal was getting closer.

"Hey pal, do you want a ride?" I looked behind me and through the snow saw a broken-down pickup truck driven by a man that looked to be First Nations. A second man was with him. Before driving me to my destination, which was a 97 Avenue trailer, the two men drove me to their reservation before taking me home. They introduced me to many of their relatives and I felt acceptance from a young boy and a wise old elder.

As the family danced and drank wine and shared with me stories of their customs, I watched in awe. Although my craving for heroin had blocked the true feeling of "love for a neighbour" that was offered to me, I sensed gladness, yes, even spurts of happiness. I realized that the two First Nations men had probably saved my life when they gave me a ride to my brother's trailer. Silently I thanked a higher power for my rescue (I didn't know Jesus then, at twenty-seven years old.) My salvation in Jesus Christ would not come for several years.

Transformation of a Hollow man

I was born on an Alberta Indian Reserve. When I was three months old, my mother left my father. My father was a rodeo circuit rider and travelled around all the time, so I was put into an orphanage. Because I was not without parents, I was not allowed to be fostered out or adopted, and I was there for six years. At age six I was placed in a detention home in Edmonton (South Side Boys Home). I was there or at an orphanage for the next four years. At the age of ten, I was sent to a reform school called Bowden Institution because I kept running away from the orphanage.

While spending four years in Bowden, I escaped numerous times. The last time was when I was fourteen years old. On this occasion, I broke into a garage to get warm. It was in the fall, and I was in pajamas. I stole nothing from the garage and left to hide under a pile of lumber in a lumber yard. Two days after my escape, I was arrested. The court system decided that I was too much for the juvenile reformatory and raised my case to adult court. At the age of fourteen and three months, I was sentenced to Prince Albert Penitentiary for two years. In this sentence, minus "good time," I was released in May 1961 free and clear.

I had found out where my dad lived and went to see him. He got me to work for him for a while, but I had a fight with his partner (who was an alcoholic and treated me like a servant). My "dad" sided with his partner, so I left. I went to New Westminster, BC, and enrolled in a special militia training program, lying about my age and background. The training program lasted six weeks. At the end of this time, it was suggested that I enlist in the regular army. I went for an interview and explained that I had a record (adult) but was only sixteen years old. They said, "Sorry, but your record excludes you from being able to join us."

I hopped on a freight train and went back to Calgary. There was nothing there for me, so I went to Edmonton. I met an acquaintance from Bowden Institution, and we (as was preordained), I guess, started to hang around together. I was a big kid, having weight lifted and shoveled coal while in the Prince Albert Penitentiary. I also trained as a boxer there. The only employment I could get was as a bouncer at an illegal poker game. I also started to roll drunks and get money any way I could.

I was depressed and was nearly killed on several occasions while rolling a drunk or just fighting. I never had any friends I could count on, so I decided to "get even." If I was going to be a crook, then I would go all the way. By all the way, I meant that I would kill someone, and from then on, I was free to do what I wanted to do. I could only hang once. When I got caught I would "spit in the eye" of the hangman and laugh at everyone.

In January of 1962 when I was in Calgary, I met a guy I had known in Prince Albert. He asked me to take care of an informer for him. He was going to court in a few days and this certain guy could sink him. I figured, "Here's my chance. I can get a real friend," so I said, "OK". My friend from Bowden Institution was with me and agreed to do it also. The man to be "taken care of" worked at a gas station, so we made it look like a robbery. My "partner" changed his mind at the last minute, but I told him someone was going to "die"; him or the informer. He didn't want to get killed, so he went along with me.

I honestly don't remember hitting the man at the service station more than once, but he was hit at least fifty times with a three-foot piece of pipe. Three days later I was picked up. I laughed at everyone. I was suddenly famous. Everybody was talking about me. I pled guilty, even though they said I couldn't do that. A capital charge had to be tried; an appeal was automatic. I was found guilty and went to Spy Hill Prison (Calgary) to wait for an appeal. My favourite song while I was there "Hang down your head, Tom Dooley." My attitude was such that the officials at the prison didn't want me there for the period between conviction and appeal, so I was transferred to Prince Albert Penitentiary to wait.

Somewhere in this process, I was told I could not be hanged. I was committed to serving a life sentence; a minimum of ten years. I went wild for a long time. I knew I would never get out, so I adjusted myself to it. I attempted to kill myself twelve times using various methods. I was considered a psychopathic killer and was treated as such. In 1965 I was transferred from Prince Albert Penitentiary to the BC Penitentiary as they had just built a special handling unit there. I was jumped, sedated, and flown from Saskatchewan to British Columbia. It took me more than three months before I knew where I was. Altogether I did six years in segregation (both in Prince Albert and BC Pen).

I met my wife while on a temporary absence from Matsqui Institution in August of 1971. I was in a pilot treatment unit (PTU), which was for drug addicts. The reason I was there was because I had not been exposed to females for so many years that I couldn't talk to women and was terrified of them. Through this PTU, I was exposed first to female nurses and then allowed escorted temporary absences. Then I was allowed unescorted absences, then work releases, and eventually, full parole in 1973.

While I was on the street I worked and supported my wife and her three children: two girls and a boy. We never got married because she wasn't sure she wanted to. I was still wild and only knew one style of life. All my friends were drug addicts or rounders. I eventually decided I wanted to do something with my life. I enrolled in five college courses and worked hard as a cement finisher. The time came when the people I was working for had finished the job in Abbotsford and had to go to the Athabasca Tar Sands in Alberta to build a recreational facility. I was given a new parole officer who would not allow me to go with the job, so I had to quit. I tried to see him, as I was upset about the whole situation, but he was too busy. I was told he went "by the book," so I could forget it.

At this time, I met a friend from the BC Pen days who was still an addict and desperate for help. I tried to find him work but couldn't. No one would listen to me. At the time he was robbing stores with a butcher knife and was desperate. So, because he was a friend, I got involved with him. I was mad at everyone and felt that no one really cared anyway. My girlfriend wouldn't marry me, and I couldn't afford to complete my college courses, so I decided to help my friend.

I started to organize and plan bank robberies. I made sure that I always held the gun so I could control the situation. I needed my gun more for controlling my partners than for the robbery. We robbed several banks, and no one was ever hurt. My philosophy was that if the police caught us I would "go down in the street with a gun in each hand".

I was eventually caught, of course, and went to court in 1975. I received an additional twenty-year sentence. My wife stayed with me, and we were married in the prison system on May 22, 1977. I was continually told that I would never get out, or at least, it would be many years before

I was considered for parole again. My wife got tired of my attitude, and I guess having to visit me regularly, and she decided to take a rest from me to consider what was ahead for her in life. I broke and lost control of my body. I knew that I would kill myself if I went into a cell one night, so I requested to be put into hospital and watched. By my appearance they knew I was serious, so the officers complied with my request.

I was at the bottom of my life. I was desperate from loneliness like I had never been before. I had, of course, heard of "Jesus" and what He could do. But I always knew I was too bad for Him. As a last resort, I cried out to Him and begged Him to take control of my life. He did. I was immediately calm and not lonely anymore. I have never been lonely since that time and have changed dramatically.

Within three years I was released on full parole. My wife and I are happily married. We still have our "ups and downs" of course, but we are happy. I have gotten employment which satisfies my need to help people who are in, or near, the same position I have been in. I did not get parole because I am a Christian but because of the change in my whole being. It was obvious to all who met me. The transformation was staggering. The things I felt contributed to my present position in life, are (1) Becoming a Christian, (2) My wife and family, (3) Attending university within prison, (4) Being given the chance to help others, (5) Being able to internalize; that I am responsible for the things I do, (6) Knowing that it is OK, even if I still make mistakes, and (7) Having someone to talk to if I need help. If I can do it so can others. I wish to emphasize that turning my life around was in spite of the of the prison system and not because of it.

One last thought for all to consider, not only for themselves, but for their families, "There but for the grace of God, go I, or mine." I fully support the Connection to Freedom.

By Tejuanis "Butch" Cassidy
Re-published 8/20/23.

See the advice given on the next page.

Message to Lifers

Don't give up; there is hope. I served twenty-three years in federal prisons and eight years in reformatories. "Prison walls do not a prison make."

There is freedom in helping other people to not have to go through what you and I have. The experience of being in jail can be a training ground to prepare for helping those who may be headed down the same road.

The best way to learn is to teach. Drugs and alcohol are an escape from reality and leave you with dirty side effects.

The Lord is an escape to the purest form of reality and Jesus doesn't leave a bad taste in your mouth. Jesus is higher than any drug can ever take you. After a dozen attempts at the "great escape" (suicide attempts), Jesus saved me from certain death. I believe fully in what Connection to Freedom is doing.

Tejuanis "Butch" Cassidy

Note

When I spoke with Tejuanis "Butch" Cassidy and his wife, on November 19, 2022, I was reminded how many years we three had known each other, and how I received his testimony in 1988 when I visited him at his home in Nanaimo. But the one thing that I cherished all these years was how he and his wife each gave me a scripture for the Connection to Freedom book. Both verses served me well.

Butch, well Tejuanis, is probably unaware that his testimony "Transformation of a Hollow man" was read in the Republic of China at a Recovery Center, by women in recovery from morphine addiction, a Chaplain at Halifax Regional Correctional Centre who thanked us on behalf of the inmates, staff, and himself for the Connection to Freedom book. A similar response came from a Chaplain at the Texas Department of Corrections who had also read the book, and in his warm letter of response encouraged us to continue.

My reason for writing about this time in all our lives, as was Tejuanis "Butch" Cassidy's hope, and purpose for sharing his testimony is to offer you who are in prisons, despite how long your sentence may be, or how seemingly hopeless your situation, Jesus Christ can and will transform your life if you say, and mean it, "help me Jesus!" - author

"Writing a Letter" Exercise

There was a time when I was in jail, and I wasn't receiving any letters. I was tired of never answering when a guard walking by my cell, never had any mail for me. I had forgotten how to write a letter. But I wrote a bunch of information. Then I mailed it to myself. One morning I heard the guard say "Bradley, mail!" But that day when I received my own letter, I felt like part of humanity, once more. I wanted to write letters, but I had forgotten how. Also, I didn't want to ask for any paper to practice. Because I'd be expected to post a letter, at least that's what I thought.

Do you want to practice writing a letter before you send it? No ideas? Here's a few: employment when you are released, a place to stay, a letter of forgiveness, a letter to your family, to your loved one, letter to your relationship, your spouse, a letter of apology, a letter to your church, or a church, a letter to your recovery group, or a recovery group, a halfway house. And of course, a letter about completing your education, if that is your need. Only you know what is important in your life.

My Practice Letter(s)

_____

_____

_____

_____

_____

_____

_____

_____

_____

_____

_____

_____

_____

Then you will call upon Me and go and pray to Me, and I will listen to you. Jeremiah 29:12

My Testimony of Forgiveness

I remembered a correctional officer long ago who accused me of using the medication I received for my epilepsy, just "to party." He didn't believe I had epilepsy. I was twenty-four years old when I had my first epileptic seizure! Here is my story:

I had recently been fired from a job because they found out I had a criminal record. I felt angry and depressed, and I couldn't stop thinking about how unfair it was when a guy is willing to live the straight and narrow, to get fired! I had drunk alcohol, and a few days previous had shot heroin. I didn't feel well, and the worst was a headache so bad it hurt like a chisel going through my brain.

I decided to go and buy some aspirin at the corner store. I had walked about half a block when suddenly I tripped, and the road seemed to rush up to my face! I tried to stand, but like a drunk (although I was completely sober) I couldn't get my footing. I lost my vision and then it was back but very blurred. I tried once more to get my footing but slipped again, and like a fish out of water, I was flopping uncontrollably. Next, I was lying in a ditch at the side of the road. Relief washed over me as I saw what I believed was my front door—the one I had just walked out of and onto the road.

Strangers came out of the driveway and there was more confusion. I attempted to tell them they were living in my home and that they'd got the wrong house, but they seemed to be saying it was me who had the wrong address. Continuing to walk the road like a drunken sailor, I saw two dark figures walking toward me from a white box-shaped object. It turned out they were ambulance attendants walking from an ambulance. I felt terrified! The next thing I became aware of was a voice questioning me: "What is your name?" I replied, "S ... t ... e ... v e." A man in white, who I assumed to be a doctor, asked my last name. I struggled and heaved in my chest; my throat was trying to form words. My memory did not allow any information to pass through my mouth. My brain was telling me in spurts, that if I didn't get the right answer, they would lock me up somewhere.

I had enough on the ball to start guessing my last name, hoping I would get it right by fluke. The doctor obviously saw right through me and within minutes I was in a wheelchair, being pushed down the hospital corridor to one room then another. I had wires and electrodes attached to my head and went through a type of hallucinogenic "trip." Then it was on to the second room where my brain was scanned by a machine. These procedures were an EEG and Brain Scan. The third room I was wheeled to had four beds and one patient whose face was badly bruised and cut.

My first thought was he had taken a beating and then after hitting the ground, been kicked in the head a few times. As the attendant was helping me get into the bed next to the patient's bed, the beaten-up man spoke, and what he said shook me: "What brings you to the epilepsy ward?" Before I could even try to speak, he continued, "They've been trying to get my epileptic seizures under control for a year, but I end up having seizures and banging my head when I fall. I always get bruised, and my face gets cut and scraped because of my seizures!"

While I was denying the fact that I too was an epileptic at the mercy of grand mal seizures, he said something that unnerved me even further: "You see the wooden stick taped to your bed above the pillow?" I looked and nodded yes. He said, "All of the beds on this ward have them. They are called tongue depressors and nurses use them if we have a seizure while we are here in the hospital. They press our tongues to the side of our mouths, so we don't choke!" I had no experience with seizures as this was only my first. I didn't know if the patient knew what he was talking about. But he'd had the seizures, and his doctors couldn't get them under control. He later admitted to me that he was taking Dilantin and Phenobarbital. These pills were commonly prescribed for epileptics at that time, 1972. He also admitted that he had been drinking beer. "I'm an alcoholic they tell me. They say drinking beers with my pills keeps me having seizures. I don't believe it though!" A week later I was leaving the hospital, confused and scared, with feelings of hopelessness dragging me down. A nurse tried to cheer me up. "There's no reason you can't lead a normal life with medication. You should not use alcohol and you cannot drive until you have been legally declared seizure-free. Your doctor will explain all these things to you."

As I walked into my doctor's office a few days later, I had made up my mind not to stop drinking but to maybe taper off a bit. Looking very serious my doctor said, "You've been diagnosed with grand mal epilepsy.

I believe this is a delayed result of your California accident." (I did not divulge my suicide attempt). My doctor was writing on his prescription pad. He said, "Take these two pills together. One is an anti-seizure drug called Dilantin and the other is a barbiturate called Phenobarbital. The pills work together. And whatever you do, don't drink alcohol while taking these.

"How long will I have to take this medication?" It seemed the obvious question, me being an alcoholic. His answer stunned me! "You'll probably have to take the pills for the rest of your life, Steve. At least until your seizures stop! You cannot legally drive an automobile until you have been medically confirmed 'seizure-free'. And I know you sometimes work construction; you cannot climb above twenty feet. Not until we see how the medications affect you!"

For the first two or three years I felt very uncertain walking on any sidewalk. I was afraid that I would, out of the blue, fall and smash my head. I would be shopping with my lady and have a seizure in a coffee shop, the coffee went flying. I was eating supper with my girlfriend and my mother when my head snapped back, and I shot forward and had a seizure!!!

I have developed the following exercise for workbook participants, because over the years, the process was of help to me. That is until I met Jesus Christ, in my cell at VIRCC, and forgave the correctional officer who didn't believe I had epilepsy. Then Peter came to Him and said, "Lord, how often shall my brother sin against me, and I forgive him? Up to seven times?" Jesus said to him. "I do not say to you, up to seven times. But up to seventy times seven." Matthew 18:21-22

I forgave my kidnapper

I was speaking with a high school class in Victoria when my thoughts carried me into the pain and heartache of my life: In a month Watts County, Los Angeles, would explode with their race riots! This was in my thoughts as homeless, I lay broken, bloody, near death after a car ran over me and left me to die. Before I was run over my last thoughts were of an African American family I had helped in Victorville's 'Shanty town.' And of the bullies who threatened to bury me in the desert who had also mocked me for my relationship with a Mexican girl.

Thanks to two sailors from China Lake Base, a California Highway Patrol officer, named Ralf Johnson, ambulance attendants and Dr Robert Hamblin, and his team at Ridgecrest Community Hospital, my life was spared. But the next day, July 5th, the newspaper, 'The Bakersfield Californian' reported a doctor's comments about me: "Bradley's badly battered body", and doctors say: "Bradley will not last the night." I recall overhearing doctors say, "It is no good putting a splint on his leg, he won't last the night!"

The consequence of my attempt to kill myself was addiction to the pain treatment morphine. Likewise at Kern County General Hospital, and after air ambulance, the Royal Jubilee Hospital in Victoria, my home. I left hospital a morphine addict, which would become my addiction to heroin, jails, and institutions. At 24, Epileptic seizures sidelined me! Fear, uncertainty, hopelessness was all I knew when my doctor said he was going to place me on Dilantin and Phenobarbital, "for the rest of your life!" When I asked how I became an epileptic, the doctor replied, "It's delayed result of your California road accident!" I had never told him it was my suicide attempt.

The reason for my suicide attempt, one month before my 19th birthday, was not racist bullies, it was the abuse I had suffered at the hands of my kidnapper when at 17, I was hitchhiking, near Stave Lake, BC, Canada.

Throughout my life to 41 years old, I would attempt suicide several times, and the reason would always be my kidnapping and the abuse I suffered, but I would blame it on other situations and circumstances, and always it would be the abuse I had received at the hands of my captor, when I was 17.

Present that day was Aneil (pastor of Connection to Freedom Community Church), the schoolteacher, and the new chair of the Camosun College Criminal Justice Program. It was my 12th annual talk at the school, and four years prior, my 10th annual talk with Camosun College Criminal Justice Program students. Not once during my many years of talks had I referred to my kidnapping and abuse when I was 17.

Although my kidnapper was probably 110 years old if he was still alive, as a memory I had kept him alive by my unwillingness to forgive. But there in front of the teachers and students, as a Christian, I forgave "the man who had all but destroyed my life!"

My sincere thanks to Pastor Aneil because, as my co-speaker his support gave me the encouragement for the very first time anywhere, to share the pain of my kidnapping and abuse.

And I was reminded of how a First Nations grandmother, and grandson, who through their compassion, had saved my life that terrible night.

I forgave my dad for his abuse!

As far back as I can remember, with racial slurs my dad had cursed every nationality but his own white Anglo-Saxon. I was eight years old, and my brother was three years younger. Mom was working afternoons as a hospital nurse. Dad had come home and was in a terrible mood after he read the note that mom had left for him about the rent.

Dad asked me where the envelope with the rent money was. I didn't know. When my younger brother said he had seen me burn some papers in the stove (which was garbage), dad hit me until my nose was bloody and my eyes were swollen. Although there were times when mom tried to intervene, she always told me, "Your dad can't help it because he's got a 'violence sickness.'"

The rent money was found after mom got home. At fourteen, my hands trembled like an old man's after a particularly vicious beating that dad gave me for missing school. I had a black eye and badly bruised ribs that he had given me.

But by far the worst violence inflicted upon me was when I was fifteen. Because mom had bought me a shirt without asking dad's permission, he ripped the shirt off my back and as if I was a full-grown man, he punched me in the head until I lost consciousness, and after I hit the ground, he kicked me (I was told by a neighbour who saw the insanity).

Dad never allowed me to invite my friends over, and mom just didn't invite her neighbour friends to visit. I always made supper as mom worked afternoons as a nurse. Once, the supper was not to dad's liking, so he screamed at me, and then with my meal, he locked me in the bathroom.

On the other hand, one day after school when I had just turned sixteen my dad was threatening to "give me a beating" and I saw red and exploded! The years that he had abused me came flashing through my mind. I grabbed him by the front of his shirt, dragged him to the top of the basement stairwell and threw him down the stairs. He fell hard on the basement floor. Looking up at me sheepishly, he invited me to "continue this fight." An overpowering desire to kick him in the head was tempered when I said, "No thanks, dad, you win!"

Never again did my dad raise his hand to me, not because he was afraid of me but because he suddenly became ill. Weeks later mom told me that dad was dying of cancer, specifically, leukemia which is cancer of the blood. He died several months later. Never will I forget whenever he was angry with me, he would yell, "You'll be in jail by the time you are nineteen!"

All my life I was unable to forgive my dad for his abuse. But thanks to my friend and social worker, Reima-Lee, who pointed me in the right direction, in 2010 I forgave him. -author

"My Forgiveness" Exercise

It is important that you understand this exercise cannot be completed in a day and probably not in a week. It may take at least a month, but it could take six months or a year or even longer. The main thing is the more you write about your feelings, the more you will learn about yourself. Do not use full names in this exercise. Example: John Smith would be "J" or "S" and Mary Jones would be "M" or "J." You may have unforgiveness (repressed anger) for more than one person. But deal with one unforgiveness at a time.

Directions: Begin by filling in the blank "I have unforgiveness for_____. But I am willing to think about why I am holding on to that unforgiveness. So, in my writing, I hope to understand.

My
Unforgiveness_____

_____

_____

_____

_____

_____

_____

My
Forgiveness_____

_____

_____

_____

_____

_____

"Therefore, if anyone is in Christ, he is a new creation; old things have passed away; behold all things have become new." 2 Corinthians 5:17

Aneil's calling by God

After holding a Connection to Freedom meeting at the Salvation Army ARC, I was on my way home, when at the front desk, I met Aneil. He asked about our meeting, and I encouraged him to attend sometime. I told him that we were a Christian addiction recovery meeting that uses the bible. It was Friday night and for several years we had held meetings there.

During one of our groups, I was surprised but blessed by the appearance of Aneil. It was Thursday night when we borrowed space from the Mustard Seed. I could not explain why, but I felt the Lord wanted me to keep an eye on Aneil and to help him whenever he needed guidance or other support.

Nevertheless, with every regular weekly Connection to Freedom meeting at the Mustard Seed, our friendship grew as did Aneil's willingness to "live for God." I saw the love he had for his mother, and I appreciated meeting her, a brave sister in the Lord.

The proof of Aneil's allegiance to the Lord began to show in his actions. No, he wasn't perfect, and neither am I, but I was convinced of his love for Jesus Christ. He became a board member of our non-profit organization. But then in mid-May 2014, I was hospitalized for a week at the Royal Jubilee after suffering a heart attack! Upon my release, I was feeling very weak. Aneil was there to support me. He even washed my dishes for me. To me, it seemed almost a given that Aneil should take over the Connection to Freedom meetings, so I could concentrate on getting well. And, in my prayers, I asked God for His will about whether Aneil should replace me as God's Connection to Freedom facilitator.

With Aneil as my co-speaker, I fulfilled a previous commitment to speak with the Law 12 students at Parkland Secondary School. The date was June 4, 2014. By His Spirit, the Lord revealed that He had chosen Aneil to carry the torch of Connection to Freedom. And God's will for me was that after twenty-five years of service to Jesus Christ, as a group facilitator, I was to retire.

With humility and gratitude, Aneil agreed to replace me and carry the torch. Almost immediately I recognized, and told him so, that God was going to use him in a bigger way than he could even imagine. Those which were once Connection to Freedom meetings, through the Lord in Aneil's life, were the beginnings of something new: invitations to guest speakers. He not only celebrated my birthday with his group, but I spoke there three times after Aneil invited me. I felt blessed to receive those opportunities to share my testimony with scripture.

The Lord it appeared had plans for Aneil, and so my friend and brother in the Lord, relocated to Duncan which is about thirty-five miles north of Victoria. It was there that Aneil was challenged because of his faith in Jesus Christ, but he grew in his faith because of this and was making God's word his life priority.

Aneil kept the name Connection to Freedom, but it was not a Connection to Freedom meeting for addicts and ex-offenders, this was "a community" of men, women, youth, and children: A fellowship, Connection to Freedom Community Church. On March 11, 2022, Aneil became a pastor to which I say praise God! Yesterday, September12, 2022, while speaking with Pastor Aneil by telephone, I let him know of the changes that I saw God making in his life. "Don't forget," he said, "you mentored me for eighteen months." Once again, I say, praise God!

Pastor Aneil's Story (rehab!)

I graduated from secondary school in Victoria. I am a third generation Victorian. My grandfathers (two) came to the city in 1910. By all accounts, I grew up living in a very loving, normal family environment. I was the eldest of two. My sister was five years younger than me. Like many young boys of my age, I idolized my father who many people said, "had charisma".

My mom, there could be no better. She loved everybody and everybody loved her. The only flaw she may have had is that her son (me) could do nothing wrong. I was not complaining. I had many of my father's traits, for the only grandma I knew. I was by far her favourite grandchild. She had thirty grandchildren. Yes, you are right, I was spoiled rotten which really is not an advantage. My ego was so big it probably could have had its own council member.

Before I was a teenager two tragic events happened in my so-called perfect life. I was molested several times by an in-lawed uncle and my father passed. Those wounds (so I was to find them later) stayed with me for over thirty years. Even with the passing of my father, my mom was a rock. She stayed a single mother dedicated to her children's well-being. About two years before my dad died, my mother became a born-again Christian. Her immediate family, which consisted of ten siblings, was shocked, but my grandma (her mom) a devout Sikh, stopped speaking to her. Through all these hardships, mom found solace in her love for Jesus Christ. Both I and my sister became Christians shortly after the death of my father. Even though as a family we attended church, I hated it!

My school years were great even with this hidden pain. I excelled in both sports and academics, was extremely popular, and had a hot car and many girlfriends. With all this I was happy; whatever I wanted I got it! My behavior was that of a deeply hurt person. I treated my so-called friends like royalty. I always bought my girlfriends. Well, I was a jerk. I showed off! I bragged even in school and the staff let things slide for me, all the time. Hey, I was the captain of three or four major sports.

All my uncles, aunts, and cousins thought I was doing well. Every summer I worked for my uncle (who for many years I idolized). To all my family I was destined for success. There was no doubt! I had many of my father's attributes plus I was learning my uncle's business. My mom taught me well and I never drank or did drugs, UNTIL! I was sixteen. Man, I loved to party!

With my loud personality, I could show off! Be the life/jackass of the party! I smoked pot every day for eleven years. I was stoned all day at school. Even before I played sports, I was stoned before every game. I felt I played better! And I did! Man, I had weed 24/7! Hey, even I knew I was going to be rich and successful! I had everything, so I thought! Even getting in five car accidents in my first Grade 12 year did not faze me. There were some concerns when I drove drunk through a basement window, but of course not by me. I knew I would get off. I did!

Over eight years, I lost my license five times and continued to drive. I failed Grade 12 on purpose to party and play sports one more year. I transferred to another school, and I was an instant hit! I was working for my family and selling weed on the side. My grades took a dip, but I was still an extremely good athlete and made it through to graduation. After I graduated, I went to work full-time for my family. Sales were my game, and I knew I was good, still smoked pot every day but slowed down on the drinking. I was living the dream, bought my first house and was making huge money. I turned twenty-one.

The party rose to a whole new level, Las Vegas! Wow! My kind of city! Two of my cousins and I flew down monthly. I had found a new passion VEGAS where I felt like a KING! My relationship with my uncle at work was dwindling. We argued so much (even though I was his top salesperson); he managed to fire me and hire me back six times.

Now, at twenty-six years old, I wanted to make more money, and even though I loved my uncle, at the same time, I despised him! Playing lacrosse, I blew out my knee. In an instant my lacrosse days were done! I would have surgery and wait a minimum of one year to heal.

With this extra time, I enrolled to acquire my real estate license. A year later, I told my uncle I was leaving. He was shocked! To this day whenever I see him, he reminds me, "You could have had all this!"

I jumped into real estate and was an instant success! But I wanted more money! I wanted to prove to my family I could be successful without their help. I knew two guys that had drug connections in Mexico for cocaine;

they needed me to be the money man, no problem. I was now in a power position, which I relished. The biggest flaw I had was I loved to be "the man." The power was going to my head, nothing could stop me, but then I decided to do some coke. I absolutely loved it! Little did I know this was the beginning of the end.

I still managed my job as a real estate agent because of all the connections I had and the money still coming in from the drug business. I knew I was hooked and in trouble, but I was still surrounding myself with many superficial friends. I really did not like myself, and I treated people like second-class citizens.

The backbreaker of all the drug use came on a two-week binge when my cousin at age thirty-two (the same age as me) started to have multiple heart attacks. We were in a hotel in Vancouver with two of his buddies. I grabbed all the remaining dope! We had called a cab and gave them a considerable sum of money to call an ambulance, and I got out of there! I just wanted to get "high"!

Two days passed, and I was out of dope, so I wanted to find out what happened to my cousin. I learned he was in the hospital fighting for his life in a coma. In shock, my drug use now had become apparent to my whole family. COCAINE was the most important thing in my life, more important than my cousin's life, which he lost three months later. That hit me hard! I was no drug dealer, not really, I only had one customer and that was me!

My mom, who never left my side, and believed in me, kept saying, "You're running from God, but He has a hold on you. One day, son, he's going to use you!" Even then I knew she was right. I wanted so desperately to find peace of mind. I decided a few days after my cousin's funeral to get back into the family's good books. I would go to rehab. My mom was supportive and sent me down to California for rehab.

I completed the program, but within three days I was all whacked out again. I would go back to treatment another three times, come out clean and sober for a bit, then relapse.

I was set up in the fast-food business and did very well for a bit, but I had not dealt with my inner issues of why I didn't like myself. Clean and sober, I was looking good on the outside, but inside I had anger issues that I did not want to deal with. I could not look at myself in the mirror.

Eventually, the business went down. Each time I relapsed; the progression of my addiction got worse. I was now a full-time crack addict!

Girls would come and go, many of them not addicts, and they just wanted to help. As an addict all I did was "TAKE," and I was such a good talker! I used everyone I could, especially my mom. Eventually that money train would dry up!

Back to rehab, I went to treatment number five, and as always, I was popular, not looking at my issues, but hey! I was clean and sober. There I met a girl, and we moved in together, to Victoria. As always, things started out great. My family bought me a brand-new truck and I went back to work for them. It did not take long for two addicts living together to get back onto the dope. Three years later my girlfriend was gone, my family decided to FIRE me again, and I had a huge crack habit. Nothing had changed because I hadn't. My addiction was so big it outweighed my money coming in.

I was hopeless, or so I thought, with nothing left in the tank. It was then on February 8 that I begged to go to treatment. For the first time, I had really had enough! I went to treatment and worked hard. Every morning and night I asked God to set me free of my addictions. I left a changed person! Finally, I had stopped this insane living! I learned in rehab that addiction was 15 percent addiction and a whopping 85 percent behaviors.

I would soon find out my anger towards being molested and my father's death would play a large role in why I could not cope with 'day to day' living. I got back to Victoria and found myself a job working for a church.

I never felt it was work—I LOVE PEOPLE—and helping them felt amazing. I felt I was finally there, becoming the person God intended me to be! I was clean and sober and my love for people and God showed. It was better than any drug I have ever done. All my friends (real ones) were coming back; I could not have been happier! I give great thanks to my mom for supporting me when I felt unlovable, through her Christian faith. Without God's love, and my mother's support, I would not be clean of a seventeen-year crack-cocaine habit.

My behavior in the last year has totally changed. My anger rarely comes up, and the real key is to never overact. For if you overact you will always regret it. I never judge anyone, never gossip, and ask God for help "one day at a time." I love Jesus Christ and helping others through Him. Thanks to the help I got from Connection to Freedom meetings.

Write me a letter if you like. I'd be glad to hear from prisoners. Or to meet with you when you are released or paroled. See the back of the book for the address. Meanwhile, here is a **Bible Study**.

-Pastor Aneil

Re-published March 27, 2024

Bible Study Exercise

Whether you are alone, or in a group, before you begin, please take a moment to thank the Lord Jesus Christ, and ask for His wisdom and understanding. **Directions:** Read the question, then from your Bible, write your answer.

(1) What is faith? Hebrews 11:1

Answer _____

_____

_____

(2) Why should I forgive somebody I hold unforgiveness for? Mark 11:25-26

Answer _____

_____

_____

(3) Why should I get baptized? Mark 16:16

Answer _____

_____

_____

(4) I've tried to live up to the Ten Commandments, you know, don't do this, and that, but no matter how strong my will, I keep failing, why? Romans 13:8-10

Answer _____

_____

_____

(5) Why should I give a tithe to my church? 2 Corinthians 9: 6-8

Answer _____

_____

_____

(6) What should I do to take a stand against evil? Ephesians 6:11-13

Answer _____

_____

_____

(7) What if I know that tomorrow will bring me temptation? Matthew 6:34

Answer _____

_____

_____

(8) "drunkenness, …. and the like" (could this mean today's fentanyl?) Galatians 5:21

Answer _____

_____

_____

(9) What made Samuel displeased? 1 Samuel 8:6

Answer _____

_____

_____

(10) What is the significance of the rainbow in Genesis 9:12-17?

Answer _____

_____

_____

(11) What is the "fear" of the Lord? Job 28:28

Answer _____

_____

_____

(12) Who signed the decree against prayer, in the 6th chapter of Daniel?

Answer _____

_____

_____

(13) What is the meaning of the vision in Amos 8:2?

Answer _____

_____

_____

(14) In Isaiah 40:31 what are the benefits to wait on the LORD?

Answer _____

_____

_____

(15) Genesis 3:1 says: "Now the serpent was more cunning than (what?)"

Answer _____

_____

_____

And those who know Your name will put their trust in You; for You, Lord, have not forsaken those who seek You. Psalm 9:10

"Faith, or fentanyl?"

I was a heroin addict for 18 years, and briefly during my early days, a dealer. Jails and institutions, empty promises, broken dreams, horrendous cold turkey withdrawals, guns, and violence were my experiences. "Chicken one day, feathers the next" was how I lived and several attempts at suicide. Near suicide in my cell at the Vancouver Island Regional Correctional Centre, and intervention by Jesus Christ, when I called out to Him, was my saving grace. From that point on I chose a clean and sober life.

God's grace, prayer, and His word, since, have transformed me from a "no good dirty junkie" as I was called by the police who smashed through my front door in search of my stash, to an advocate for those who suffer and high school students, so they didn't have to, and 'addiction and criminality' talks for Camosun College Criminal Justice students.

In early 2022 however, I was shocked to hear the number of overdose deaths, many from fentanyl, in British Columbia, and I was reminded of my attendance at Victoria City Hall in the mid-nineties, when Chief Coroner, Vince Cain, led a forum, titled, "Drug Deaths in BC."

The first to speak was a grandfather who was clutching a framed picture of his 21-year-old grandson. The young man had experimented with heroin and died from an overdose. Wracked with grief, the grandfather was trembling with anger, as tears welled up in his eyes. "How could this have happened? My grandson wasn't a street kid! How did he get hold of heroin?"

I had attended the forum with my friend who was the Director of the Methadone Clinic, and a Clinic doctor, holding her newborn baby. Perhaps I was thinking of that baby growing up in a world of "drugs" or "to do the right thing" in front of my friend from the Clinic, but more likely, out of feelings of guilt and shame, having once been a dealer, I stood up.

Facing the grandfather, awkwardly I said: "Heroin is easy to get for anybody. It's on the streets all over! You don't have to be in the know! Anybody who wants it can get it! Sometimes the heroin is "peppered with" "stepped on" that is, "laced with" a poison, to give the heroin a more powerful "rush" with the first injection!" Chek TV, filmed my story, adding to my shame and guilt, and deep regret.

23 years later, 2017 to be exact, with my friend Dr. Robert Hamm, a physician, by invitation from Aneil who now pastors the Connection to Freedom Community Church, in Duncan, I attended another forum. This was facilitated by a woman who was an advocate for 'parents who had lost one or more siblings' to opioid overdose deaths.

As the grandfather had done 23 years earlier, she too held a framed picture of her son, in his 20's. The young man had experimented with heroin, just like the grandson, so many years earlier. It was thought when he died from an overdose, that heroin was the cause. But an autopsy revealed that he died from an overdose of fentanyl.

The advocate, grieving, although energetic, spoke to us 40 audience members of which some were practicing drug addicts. The mother announced, "If you think fentanyl is going away sometime, forget it! Fentanyl is here to stay! And it is getting worse!"

For a moment I asked myself, if I had done anything to help the community, to get a handle on illicit drugs. A memory flashed back.

In 2001, for a year Kurt, my co-worker and I had facilitated a Connection to Freedom meeting at Vancouver Island Regional Correctional Centre and for almost 6 years at the Needle Exchange. We were a Christian non-profit society, and I was the facilitator of the meetings under that umbrella which was for addicts and ex-offenders, street addicts, and others.

The mother who was dealing with the grief of losing her son, through advocacy, spoke: "If you use illicit opioids, like fentanyl, make sure you don't use them alone. If you do use opiates, make sure you have a Naloxone Kit with you. This is an opioid overdose reversal spray. But it won't do you any good unless you know how to use it. They are offering training at Aids Vancouver Island!"

I was happy to hear that Pastor Aneil, and his team, in 2021 had provided instruction sessions on the use of the Naloxone kits, at his Duncan based Connection to Freedom Community Church.

A student from Victoria high school where I had spoken sent me an e-mail. She had an accident and was afraid of taking morphine. She didn't want to become addicted to morphine. The student didn't want to become a heroin addict. With assurance and the fact that I was not qualified to give medical advice, only to tell my story, she thanked me.

Faith in Jesus Christ, prayer, and God's word gave me the power to overcome my 18 years addiction to heroin, and other opioids! As the Bible says in Matthew 6:34 'one day at a time'.

Parole Hearing and Group Insight

I had briefly worked as night staff at the Salvation Army Addictions Recovery Centre, and the Manchester House for federal parolees. I appreciate both opportunities. I remember through Connection to Freedom meetings. The following is a Parole Hearing that I attended.

This inmate had reached out to me with his letters and had written and donated a poem which I had published in one of my books. He had also sent me a copy of his story which I found amazing. However, because his dad had been a strict preacher, the inmate had no tolerance for any recovery programs that were based on Christ such as our 'Connection to Freedom' meeting. I visited the inmate a couple of times, and I was impressed by his straightforward answers to any of my questions. But he was not the only inmate who was reaching out to me, and my visits to meet with the parole candidate came to an end. However, not before I told him of my willingness to support him at his hearing.

Unaware that one day he would share his story as my co-speaker, at the Camosun College for the Criminal Justice Program, when I attended his Parole Hearing I brought a copy of my book to help 'at risk youth' and pointed to the inmate's poem that he had sent me. I also found out that he was a prolific writer regarding addiction and recovery. He was well spoken and well educated, and I felt that he certainly had a good program back into the community on parole. With stipulations that he attend the 'Connection to Freedom' meetings, and /or other groups, he was paroled.

The parolee settled in the community quite well and he kept his appointments with his parole officer, we met for coffee regularly, and a few times we met at my home. Meanwhile, he was working toward courses at Camosun College. But he also began to talk about the probability that he was going to relocate to Vancouver. I began to feel uneasy, but he had impressed me with his knowledge about recovery from addiction, and his spiritual understanding of a concept, not a God, that was needed for his recovery. But the parolee had come to one meeting of 'Connection to

Freedom' only and assured me that he was going to NA meetings for his drug problem.

At first, he and I phoned each other, he from Vancouver and me from Victoria. His terrific sense of humor always lifted me, and I encouraged him on his recovery walk. The day that he was accepted for classes at Vancouver College, I was sure he was on his way to success. By then we were the best of friends, and our phone calls defined our relationship as he called us "brothers in recovery". Once more he referred to NA as his regular meeting.

I became busy presenting school talks, "bible counseling" with a William Head Institution parolee, preparations for 'Connection to Freedom' meetings, and a homeless man was meeting with me regularly, to learn how the bible could help him. The parolee over in Vancouver although in my thoughts, and hopes for him, I did not think to phone him. I believed with his last report that his life was orderly, and his recovery meeting was regular. At least the last time I spoke with him on the phone that is how it sounded to me. I was confident that the parolee, "my friend" was doing OK. Without a care in the world, under bright sunshine I was downtown when I ran into someone I knew from our group. He asked if I had heard anything about the guy that I had supported from VIRCC who made parole. My stomach tightened and my throat became dry as I expected the worst. "He was found dead of a heroin overdose in downtown Vancouver!" It was true. I felt sick with grief for some time, but then Kurt and I were invited to hold Connection to Freedom meetings at the Vancouver Island Regional Correctional Centre. The following will explain:

Through Christ I introduced a man to Jesus Christ, attended his court hearing and sentencing on a 2nd degree murder and corresponded with him for quite a while. A second inmate, a big guy who had a thick Bronx, New York, accent, would never attend a Connection to Freedom meeting but every week he stopped by to say hello to Kurt, my co-facilitator, and I. A First Nations inmate whose drawing (in this workbook) donated his illustration to be used by Connection to Freedom. We used this artwork for our Connection to Freedom Jail and Street Outreach Society. The scripture above the drawing was, 'It is for freedom that Christ has set us free' Galatians 5:1

After almost a year the Connection to Freedom meetings at the prison came to an end. But then one morning I received a telephone call from Calgary. It was from a man who had attended Connection to Freedom meetings at the Vancouver Island Regional Correctional Centre. He had phoned me to ask, "How do I start up a Connection to Freedom meeting, here in Calgary?" He said the meetings had "helped him". I had given this inmate some clothing that I took to the jail before he was released and when he was set free, I took him to the Mustard Seed Street Church service. It was Sunday, after all. But I'll never forget the blessing that Kurt and I received from the Lord through presenting our Connection to Freedom prison ministry meetings.

Since the 1987 VIRCC meetings of Connection to Freedom the first meeting in the community was outside Victoria, in Langford, at the Seamen's Hall. We had rented the hall. Eleven people, some from downtown Victoria, attended through volunteer transportation. I used a bible to facilitate the group, with the assistance of Janet. A book contributor who had served time in Texas, when he read his own story for the very first time said, "I am an alcoholic!" His story is in this workbook. Looking ahead to my retirement after 25 years of facilitating Connection to Freedom meetings I am reminded of a telephone call from Los Angeles. A mother whose son had been in prison there had called to thank our group for our letters, cards, and our prayers in support of her son because he had made it to a halfway house. This list is our 25 years of letter writing to inmates:

Oakalla Prison (men) Oakalla Prison (women) Kent Institution, Matsqui Institution, Vancouver Island Regional Correctional Centre, Nanaimo Correctional Centre, Lower Mainland Regional Correctional Centre for Women, Fraser Regional Correctional Centre, William Head Institution, Mission Institution, Dorchester Penitentiary, Halifax Regional Correctional Centre, Massachusetts Correctional Institution, Lancaster State Prison, Corcoran State Prison, South Dakota State Penitentiary, Death Row-San Quentin, Idaho State Prison, Vacaville Mental Health Facility, Chuckwalla Valley State Prison and Kern Valley State Prison. A Massachusetts inmate wrote to us for five years. Although in later correspondence we found out that he had cancer. But his uplifting letters were a real blessing to our Connection to Freedom group.

Note: In Canada and /or the USA if you would like information on ministry to prisoners, or ministry to addicts, the address to send your letters is at the back of the book. -author

"Violence was an addiction to me!"

My dad, until I was 16, bullied me, kept me a frightened child with his violence, and his unreasonable beatings fueled by blind rage. Almost when it pleased him, he flipped out with no warning and went totally wild, with his fists flailing at my head and body. His shoes, once I hit the ground. I defended him to myself, convincing myself that as mom said, he can't help it your dad has a 'violence sickness' that maybe ran in his family. I lived in fear in my teen years. I shook whenever he yelled. One morning I left a note for my mom, who worked as a night nurse. With the trembling of an old man's hand, I wrote: "I feel sick mom and I can't go to school today." She wrote me an excuse that my fat lip and black eye were my fault because I had fallen down the stairs in the dark. Mom couldn't face the truth and I, being the eldest of three boys, paid for it whenever dad's violence exploded.

It happened that in high school I got into a fight with a guy who had been bullying other kids. He had tested the waters, with me, with sarcastic comments, and I did not take the bait. Then he embarrassed me in front of the entire school. I was terrified of him because he reminded me of my dad, and I really wanted to back down. But there was something inside me that would not allow me to run. I punched the guy hard until his face was swollen, and he put his hand up in surrender. With that punch to this bully's head, I was filled with glee and a huge adrenaline rush. I realized without understanding the feeling or process that brought it, in that moment, I was addicted to violence.

Throughout my later teens, twenties and thirties whenever there was a violent situation, I was drawn into it like a moth to a flame. Starting in high school, carrying on to a one night only barroom bouncer, I found violence attractive. I can't explain it, but I got a thrill from beating somebody up. There were very few nights when I was not scrapping in the bar, somewhere. Sure, alcohol would set me off into violent rages but if the violence hadn't been there inside of me already, I wouldn't have inflicted so much harm on others.

One night thinking of myself to be something, and very confident, quicker than I could blink, I lost a front tooth, and part of my hearing and walked around for a week in a daze. I had met my match in downtown Vancouver, in a bar fight. Lesson to me, violence brings only more violence! Nonetheless, I am convinced that the adrenaline rush of violence is as addictive as drugs and alcohol to addicts, like me!

The day I walked inside a jail, in 1981, I thought of how that night I would use a sheet to hang myself. A nurse at the police station had asked me if I felt suicidal and I had replied "no" with a smile and a joke. I could no longer keep up the act. I knew what I had to do. A voice from outside of my cell, a friendly tone, caused me to stand against the bars. An inmate asked me, "Hey man, do you want me to get you a sandwich and a coffee?" Four days later, however, I was throwing hot coffee at an inmate when he attempted to bully me-very common in jails. He called me "crazy!"

My insanity continued with a second violent act. I hit a man so hard I thought I'd killed him. He had been stealing from a group of fellow inmates. Anger was the feeling that I expressed freely. I believed I had the right to be angry and to re-act to the wrong against my fellow inmates and me, with no thought or consideration for anyone else's feelings. This is typical behavior behind bars. I was transferred to the Dormitory area and met a young inmate. He read his bible at night and talked to anybody who would give him their ear for five minutes about "Jesus". Me, I was getting a girl's name tattooed on my left shoulder. The design of ink was a heart with wings. This seemed to illustrate my inability to express my true feelings. There was something about the Christian kid that drew me close to him and inspired me to softer thoughts. One day the youth was attacked by some inmates. I saw red! I jumped up on a table and swinging a chunk of wood threateningly, I challenged everyone to a fight who felt like picking on the young guy and his "Jesus". I could not make any sense out of my desire to defend this youth.

On the other hand, another inmate about the same age as the Christian kid, asked me to help him. He had lost two cartons of cigarettes, betting on a football game and he couldn't pay. I refused to help him. Betting on sports, in jail, you better be able to pay, or suffer the consequences.

I received a visit from a woman who was a member of the Western Community Baptist Church. She gave me a bible signed by her and her husband. She told me that the young Christian who I had helped belonged to their church and was in a bible class there. But it wouldn't be until five years later when again in jail, I would hit rock bottom at the point of suicide and plead with Jesus Christ to save me.

Many years have passed, but through Jesus Christ, violence is no longer a part of me, as I give thanks, day by day, for my salvation. May I suggest you look, again, or for the first time, at the *Aggressive Behavior Exercise*. This was a big help to me, and others, inmates, and addicts, both in Canada and the US according to their letters.

"Aggressive Behavior!"

The Aggressive Behavior I am talking about is "violence".

It was Christmas time and I had just walked into my cell at Wilkinson Road Jail after cutting slash all day on my work gang. Before I left for work that morning I had taped a Christmas card to the dingy wall. It brightened my cell to my way of thinking. The card had a picture of a warm fire and family and a Christmas tree.

But there had been a cell inspection by the West Wing guard, and he had ripped my card from the wall, and thrown it into my toilet. I looked at the mud on my boots, and the dingy wall, and I exploded! I stormed down the tier, with my mind filled with hate, towards the guard who had destroyed my Christmas! I saw only flashes of red!!!

Just then a friend of mine called me from his cell, "What's going on with you, Steve? Here's a card for your wall!" Suddenly, it came to me! In my blind rage I could have really hurt that guard.

My thoughts shifted to my youth in Trona, California when I booted a guy in the head after I lost control. The State Police were called, and they threatened to lock me up. I was fired from my job as a handyman because of my violence. I was 18 years old.

I remembered how in Vancouver, BC, I was in my twenties. Two guys got the jump on me in an East Vancouver hotel and threw a coat over my head and punched me and kicked me until I lost my hearing temporarily, and my tooth was knocked out. I was hospitalized at St. Paul's Hospital.

On a jail sentence, in 1985, I caught an inmate stealing from other inmates and I flew into a rage! I punched the thief in the head, and blood sprayed from his mouth. All I could do was lay on my bunk seeing only flashes of red!!!

The one thing that has helped me, of course is ***Jesus Christ, and the study of God's word***. Whether you are a believer, or not, writing can help you. I began by writing a suicide note in my cell when I was 41 years old. Now I have written and published several books, including this workbook that gives you the opportunity to help yourself.

The Exercise begins on the next page.

"My Aggressive Feelings" Exercise

Directions

(1) Please underline with your pencil, anything, in the story you have just read, if it reminds you of your life. (2) From the Word List choose a word or words that describe how you are feeling this very moment. (3) Choose a word or words that describe how you have been feeling over the last seven days, or the last month. You can, if you wish, consider your writing as your recovery journal.

Word List

Annoyed, Thankful, Uptight, Uplifted, Concerned, Embarrassed, Optimistic, Stressed, Heartbroken, Peaceful, Troubled, Moody, Neglected, Ashamed, Happy, Rewarded, Proud, Impatient, Overjoyed, Suspicious, Betrayed, Prepared, Secure, Loved, Deceived, Delighted, Listless, Irritable, Hopeful, Regretful, Prayerful, Grateful, Empowered, Blessed, Motivated, Faith, Bitter, Forgiving, Dismal, Laughable, Repetitive, Heartsick, Lovable, Drained, Triggered, Calm, Acceptance, Balance, Self-compassion, Healing, Trusting, Release, Steadfast, Surrender, Frightened, Relapse, Kindness, Self-hate, Recovering, Victorious, Control, Truthful.

How I am feeling

_____

_____

_____

_____

_____

_____

_____

_____

_____

_____
_____
_____
_____
_____
_____
_____
_____
_____
_____
_____
_____
_____
_____
_____
_____
_____
_____
_____
_____
_____
_____
_____
_____
_____
_____
_____
_____
_____
_____
_____

"Do not envy a man of violence and do not choose any of his ways."
Proverbs 3:31

Christmas Raffle

Reading the newspaper one morning in early December Rej realized that Christmas was not always a happy time for Victoria's children, and single parents. Remembering that last Christmas was also very dismal for him, he set out to make the coming Christmas as bright as he could. Teaming up with Karl, another inmate. his ideas became motion. The atmosphere of VIRCC began to take on a lighter spirit as Rej, and Karl's ideas became one. Karl was a professional chef on the street, and as the inmate baker he created a "Christmas Gingerbread House" cake.

Rej who originated this project worked tirelessly for days. Using a cutting edge approximately 1 inch by 1/8th of an inch, he fashioned hundreds of tickets, he also typed and designed the tickets. By hand he wrote each ticket number. This then became a "Christmas raffle for the Gingerbread House". The tickets said, "Raffle by the Connection to Freedom Group and Residents of VIRCC".

Rej the inmate who initiated the raffle, on Sept 7th, had also given 'Connection to Freedom' as the name for our group, suggested the proceeds from the sale of the tickets should go to the "Times-Colonist, 1000 Fund". The newspaper took a great interest in this and sent a photographer to capture the wonderful event. I watched from the courtyard as this was taking place, mentally preparing myself for my Dec 17th paroled release to my brother's home.

The good energy within VIRCC began to snowball as the Inmate Committee became involved. Through his positive leadership Rej arranged to have Harvey, a former inmate return to the prison dressed as "Santa Clause". Harvey drove up to VIRCC in a Red Roadster, not a sleigh with reindeers, and visited with the children of the inmates in the visiting room. I had asked the Deputy Director if I could return to the prison as "Santa's helper" but smiling he said. "No, Bradley! Get on with your parole!"

My salvation experience

My school buddy, Ross, whom I had known since we were fourteen, shared the reason for the peace that was in him as "Jesus Christ." Asking if I would like the same inner peace in my life, I responded, "Yes!" But my old addict thinking told me this salvation experience would be like a drug "high." This was enhanced in my thoughts when I was reminded of how Ross had told me about the drugs he used when he was in university. Therefore, the inner peace that showed like a beaming red glow on his face, in my mind, was drug related.

I was mixed up and yet driven to find this wonderful inner peace. I asked Ross, "What do I do?" His response was a wide-eyed surprise that I was interested in Christ. He then became very serious and told me that I needed to "confess my sins." But to me, the word "sin" had always meant a criminal act. He was asking me, it seemed, to admit the criminal offences that I had committed.

As I sat there secretly nursing an opioid binge hangover, I asked "What sins? I've served my time, and I haven't been caught for the other sins I've done. The police just weren't fast enough!"

"Sin is not a criminal act." replied Ross, the only Christian I had ever really known. "Sin means separation from God. He knows every sin you have ever committed in your life." "Then if He already knows, why do I have to confess?" He said, "It is the way of salvation. Do you want it?"

"Yes," I said, not knowing what I was heading for. I followed him as if he was a schoolteacher and I was a schoolchild. "Lord, I confess I'm a sinner. I repent of my sins. I ask you to forgive me and to come into my life. I receive you now as my Lord and Savior." I echoed his every word expecting to feel a great big rush or the sound of trumpets.

There was nothing! I felt no change whatsoever. Nothing! I was reminded of my childhood experiences when a teacher was reading her bible to our class and called me "Thief" after money went missing. I remembered how, with God, whether I understood or not there was pain. I believed that because I had denied God for years, He was not going to allow me to be saved. I was filled with deep disappointment.

Seeing the sadness on my face, Ross, my old and wise school friend asked, "Would you like to receive the Holy Spirit?" Considering that this "Holy Spirit" was part of the salvation package, why not say "yes"? Maybe this is all that's missing? I spoke: "Yes!" Ross then placed his hand on my shoulder saying, "Fill Steve with your Holy Spirit, Lord!" From the bottoms of my feet to the hairs on my head I felt a great power surge through me. The first bible verse I read assured me in a very private and unique way that, if I now chose to live a sober life, through Jesus, I had the ability. I felt excited and hopeful. Newness had come over me and this brought a smile to my face.

But alcohol and drugs took me to the end of myself and I lived in denial of Jesus Christ. The result was jail cells and psych ward, broken relationships, and severe depression. At the point of suicide in my cell at VIRCC, after ten years of living how I pleased, I hit rock bottom and pleaded with God for His help. It was then I realized Jesus Christ had not left me nor had He forsaken me!

"Is it easy being a Christian?"

So, is there any hope for men and women who are addicted to toxic drugs? Let me ask you, are you abusing alcohol, or do you smoke too many cigarettes? Are heroin or fentanyl or other toxic drugs destroying your life? Are you sick and tired of ending up on the streets or in prison? Please keep in mind that recovery, whether from addiction, abuse, or all forms of self-abuse, is a lifetime process, and the promise of God is "being confident of this very thing that He who has begun a good work in you will complete it until the day of Jesus Christ" (Philippians 1:6).

Is it easy being a Christian? The answer is no. The difference that Jesus Christ makes in our lives, however, is that we are not alone in our struggles. We are told to expect times of trial and tribulation, but through these, we gain deeper faith and a true understanding of God's mercy, forgiveness, and grace. Do I still fall into periods of doubt and confusion? My old nature is no different than yours and your old nature and mine are no different than Paul the apostle's. Through his writings, we learn to keep focused on Christ, even when we give in to the demands of our old nature.

Paul wrote: "Not that I have already attained, or am already perfected; but I press on, that I may lay hold of that for which Christ Jesus has also laid hold of me. Brethren, I do not count myself to have apprehended; but one thing I do, forgetting those things which are behind and reaching forward to those things which are ahead, I press toward the goal for the prize of the upward call of God in Christ Jesus" (Philippians 3:12–14).

I had the privilege to share my testimony in Sunday Magazine which was our Christian community newspaper. In 2022, as I revisited my testimony, I was filled with a love for Jesus Christ that I had not previously experienced. In reading the article which was titled "Christ's forgiveness is the power that overcomes addiction" I was taken back in my mind to the years that I suffered with alcohol, drugs, cigarettes, broken relationships, and criminal activity.

I give thanks to God for His gift to me of suffering, and for His Son Jesus Christ who has set me free. My clean and sober life is based on obedience to God's word, daily. And to forgive because it is my Christian duty.

"And whenever you stand praying, if you have anything against anyone, forgive him, that your Father in heaven may also forgive you your trespasses. But if you do not forgive, neither will your Father in heaven forgive your trespasses." Mark 11:25–26.

In Christ,

Steve

"Kurt's view"

One winter evening in about 1996 I was checking the door of the Mustard Seed Street Church, and I was surprised when I found it was open. I was looking for a Bible Study group or a teaching activity where God was the focus. This was the night I met Steve who invited me to join the 'Connection to Freedom' group.

"When I met Steve, he was teaching people about self-confrontation through the Bible. He told me two of his friends who lived in Blythe, California, had taught him how to facilitate this program. This teaching was not related to 'Connection to Freedom' but it was an excellent workbook and Bible program.

I had walked the streets for years giving out gospel tracts and helped street people through a small downtown room at the corner of Yates and Douglas. I had worked in the shipyards and, whenever I got the chance, I shared Christ with my work buddies.

Steve and I became close friends and co-workers in outreach. I helped him at the Needle Exchange and was with him at the prison where we shared the Lord when holding Connection to Freedom meetings.

When Steve became a Chaplain, my wife and I asked him to perform the marriages of two of my three daughters. We were blessed by the ceremonies, and the scriptures that Chaplain Steve shared were from the 'Love Chapter' of the Bible.

Being part of the original group that formed the Connection to Freedom Jail and Street Outreach Society was a blessing I feel from the Lord.

See next page.

God's "Intervention"

First and foremost, our thanks to the board of directors and pastoral staff of Centennial United Church for loaning us a 'Connection to Freedom' meeting space and a room for my one-to-one counseling. Addiction is called "cunning and baffling" by some recovery groups. A strange disease! But at the Connection to Freedom meetings, from which I retired three years ago, we considered it to be a spiritual fight and believed the first step to recovery begins by naming addiction "a sin".

The family of the addict is forced into an "addictions pit!" The members of the family, which include from children to grandparents and everyone in between, become "infected" with the great need they feel to rescue the suffering addict, who is breaking their hearts but cannot stop his or her behavior. Addiction, "the beast within", provides no warning or signs to alert the unsuspecting. Just like a rattlesnake strikes like lightning, an opioid overdose devastates the mind and body with frightening speed. Heroin laced with fentanyl is a prime example.

A person addicted to opioids might be in their teens, in their thirties or even fifties. They often see themselves as having no serious problem but just an occasional, or perhaps even frequent, need to satisfy their craving, which they usually rationalize as "weekend recreation". Some other addicts see themselves as "victims" of an uncaring medical profession which "got them started" or of good-time party friends who had "pressured" them into taking these drugs. There are as many excuses for addiction as can be imagined by the human mind.

Several years ago, my co-worker Kurt and I were invited by a family to hold an intervention with a member of that family who was out of control with heroin and other opioids. My faith first and foremost but also my "clean" time, it was felt, would be a good influence on this addict since I too had suffered addiction to heroin until Christ saved me in my jail cell.

So, Kurt and I opened in prayer, proclaiming God's word: "For the word of God is living and powerful and sharper than any two-edged sword, piercing even to the division of soul and spirit, and of joints and marrow, and is a discerner of the thoughts and intents of the heart." Hebrews 4:12

We had faith that God would cut to the root cause of this problem, which was mainly heroin addiction, but other opioids as well. We left it up to God, having prayed and read scripture. But, at first nothing changed in this person's life. Street life again became the person's sad reality. But, at the turn of the New Year into 2017, a few years after our bible intervention, a social worker friend told me that the family member who had been struggling with heroin and opioids was now clean and sober and she was upgrading her education. "Glory to God" in His time, not ours.

Connection to Freedom workshop

I was in the middle of presenting a six-week addiction recovery program at the Hope Farm, which is in Duncan, BC. A man who was a parolee of the William Head Institution, and attended Connection to Freedom meetings, assisted me. My tools were God's word, and my 2004 book, *Connection to Freedom Addictions Recovery Workbook,* and prayer. I looked forward to these farm sessions, and the shared experiences of several group attendees. I felt comfortable and to be honest I felt comfortable in my sobriety from heroin, perhaps a little prideful also. That is until a recovering addict told his story to the group. This ended with his being near death in the hospital because of an overdose. His liver was in such bad shape that he almost died. I kept silent because his life sounded much like my own.

As if I had rehearsed to take over at the very moment, he ended his speech, I blurted out, "I don't think my liver is in very good shape! I fixed with a guy in jail, and he had the hepatitis c virus!" "Steve, you've got to get a blood test!" I responded with, "Yes, I'll see my doctor about it, thanks for your story brother!"

Days later after our Connection to Freedom meeting at the Needle Exchange I talked with the Street Nurse about a blood test. But I turned it down saying I would get the blood test at my doctor's office. The truth is, I was afraid! Not of the needle, I had used many as a heroin addict. I was terrified of finding out that my liver was destroyed, and I was dying.

When I facilitated the next Hope Farm recovery meeting, I talked with my parolee friend, and his lady, and both encouraged me to get "a blood test". The man who had shared his story with us at the previous recovery workshop, inquired how I was doing regarding a blood test.

I later spoke with a man whose parole I had supported, at the Vancouver Island Regional Correctional Centre. At different times in our lives, he and I had lived in California. He suggested I go to the doctor. For some reason, during our prayers, the Lord touched me. I knew it was time to get a blood test and following that a liver biopsy at the hospital.

During those several hours my friend prayed for me. My liver damage was on a low scale and there seemed to be no reason to worry but to use common sense, no alcohol etc.

Perhaps I took too much for granted but nearly ten years later, my doctor reported some problem with my blood. I once again started to feel afraid. But this time, I prayed, searched the scriptures, and took a three-month treatment, as delivered by two very pleasant Hep C Nurses, and a doctor, which included medication. After 90 days I received a telephone call to let me know I no longer have hepatitis C.

A doctor who knew I wrote books and had used heroin, encouraged me to tell my story as often as I could, so other drug addicts who were afraid of getting a blood test, might be encouraged to get that all important blood test.

If I had not been invited to hold a six-week addictions recovery meeting at Hope Farm, I may never have received this healing. But allow me to pass on to you these simple few words: "If you have ever used drugs by needle, even once, according to my doctor, you should GET A BLOOD TEST!

"And all things, whatever you ask in prayer, believing, you will receive." Matthew 21:22

"Bullying": by WH Parolee

Al had attended Connection to Freedom meetings regularly, sometimes with his lady friend. It was not hard to see why he was institutionalized. He had spent time in prisons back east and was now on parole in BC from the William Head Institution. I met with him on one several times, and his lady friend was a ray of sunshine to him. In fact, her nick name was "Sunshine". As was my custom, my method of counseling, to encourage men and women with broken lives to share their stories. I asked Al who was a William Head Institution parolee, if he would tell me his. And I asked him if I could write, while he talked. He scowled, grinned, and then let out a huge sigh!

"My criminal career probably started when I was 5 years old here in Victoria. I used to bully this kid at school for his lunch. I always made it like I was going to give him a beating if he never gave me his lunch. The kid just started giving me his lunch without me asking him. I saw this worked well. So, when I got to high school, I muscled kids for their cigarettes. If I never got their smokes, I would show the blade of my knife."

Al seemed to be on a roll, so I didn't interrupt him. "I got in the habit of anytime I wanted something off somebody I would make like I was going to hurt them, and that's all I had to do. I started running into older guys and I didn't always come out a winner." As I thought about Al's 26 years in prison, I sensed that he might have stabbed or shot somebody when they wouldn't hand something over that he wanted. Al didn't want to talk about his life anymore, but he said I could use what was already written, to help high school kids and so on.

A month or so later I caught Al in a pretty good mood for talking. I asked what he would say to a youth – a girl or boy-who is getting bullied? I told him it is a very serious issue: He said, "Steve, tell them not to accept it if somebody is bullying them. Hey, if it gets bad enough go and tell the teacher, or their dad or an uncle, and let them deal with it. If they can't, get a copper, a policeman!" Against his parole stipulations Al used alcohol and was sent back to prison. But, Fran, a staff member of the Mustard Seed, and I, went to William Head Institution and spoke on his behalf, Al was again released on parole.

Matsqui parolee's story

I have written this testimony for Steve of the Connection to Freedom Prison Outreach to help men who will be cut loose from prison. I am on parole now from Matsqui Prison where I was serving time for armed robbery.

I started doing time when I was 19. I grew up in the Oakalla Prison and graduated to the so-called Big Houses-William Head, Matsqui, Mission and BC Penitentiary. My testimony is not meant to be a scare tactic, it's just to make young people aware. I am writing my story for this Connection to Freedom book program, to show the hope that I am clinging to.

I came from an alcoholic home, and we moved more times than some people change their clothes. I was constantly changing schools too. None of my childhood friendships lasted because we were always on the move. I was a quiet child and always kept my feelings hidden. I ran away from home on a couple of occasions.

On one of my runaways a friend and I hitchhiked all the way across Canada, on about $150 between us. We were gone for five months. After we got back from our trip, we experimented with a bottle of wine. I loved it and the way it made me feel. When I was drinking it, I never felt alone, and my friends called me "the life of the party". I used to steal booze off my mom and dad and keep it in my locker at school. I didn't realize that this new false happiness and false courage would cost me dearly and send me to a life behind bars.

The first time I tried heroin I was behind bars. By the time I got released it was all I could think about. I went right down to the corner of Granville Street to score. I could go on and on until next week telling you about where booze and dope, including prescription drugs from doctors, led me and can lead you too.

I am now at the crossroads of my life. I never figured a guy like me would come to a time in his life when he knows he's doing the right thing. By this I mean that the right thing for me is looking for work, trying to stay straight and trying to maintain some type of relationship with God.

Since writing this brief testimony God has truly blessed my life and provided me with real joy and a reason for living". Yours in Christ, *K.H.*

Prison visits and Community

Kurt, my co-facilitator, and I, by invitation of the Chaplains at Vancouver Island Regional Correctional Centre (VIRCC), facilitated a regular, weekly Bible based Connection to Freedom meeting at the Centre. The group continued for almost a year. Upon their re-entry to the community, three inmates, now former, attended our Connection to Freedom meetings.

I received three invitations to speak about the Connection to Freedom meetings, and how William Head Institution inmates, might benefit. The third request was by invitation from the First Nations inmates to their Pow Wow. With permission from them, I invited Rev Don Isner, of Centennial United Church, and my co-worker Bev, a gentle spirited Christian. A William Head parolee attended Connection to Freedom meetings at the Mustard Seed, and Centennial United Church. The meetings were held for 15 and 5 years, approximately.

Assisted by a Parolee of Matsqui Institution, with his Parole Officer's permission, we travelled by car to Prince George, in snowy and frigid temperature there, to talk about Connection to Freedom meetings, and how this group might help them. We prayed with them, and shared Jesus Christ in our lives. At that time the inmates who were mainly First Nations, called the jail, "The Hill". Of course it is now called Prince George Regional Correctional Centre. Two members of Emmanuel Baptist Church in Victoria had sponsored us.

One evening while I was facilitating Connection to Freedom meetings at Victoria's Needle Exchange, a staff member handed me an envelope. The letter was from a Kern Valley State Prison inmate in California. Immediately I was impressed! The writer asked us to pray not only for himself, but also for his cellmate. Through transfers to other prisons such as Corcoran State Prison, and others, he and I corresponded for several years.

Through Gospel singer Germaine and Bible teacher Ben, who lived six months in Victoria and the rest of the year in Blythe, California, by correspondence I was introduced to the Christian inmates Gospel group, at Chuckwalla State Prison. Previously, Ironwood, Mule Creek,

Eagle Mountain prisons. I shared letters with California inmates for 15 years. This was of course through Connection to Freedom meetings, once monthly. During that time, our correspondence was with a Massachusetts inmate who had cancer. He was a young guy and always had something positive to say, that's why we corresponded with him for 5 years.

I recall a correctional officer from VIRCC who phoned me. He was dealing with an inmate who was suicidal. I went to the Centre, met with the inmate in his cell, prayed for him. For several years he hardly missed attending Connection to Freedom meetings at the Mustard Seed.

Whenever you hear the name 'Connection to Freedom' regarding meetings, or book, these programs were founded through Jesus Christ, and with the participation of VIRCC inmates, and a woman named Janet. "Transformation of a Hollow man" by Tejuanis Cassidy I highly recommend.

Our Youngest Member

I had spent time in God's word and established my message. That day I had made photocopies of my scriptures and a prayer sheet. I thought about last week's group, and how after prayerfully opening the Connection to Freedom meeting, we sometimes sang a hymn. Occasionally, a group member brought a guitar. This testimony is about one such person.

As I had for more than half a dozen years at the Salvation Army, Friday evenings, I took the elevator to the meeting room. Prayerfully I waited for the Connection to Freedom members and first-time attendees to show up. It might be a federal parolee, an ex-inmate of VIRCC, a street guy addicted to rubbing alcohol, an ex-biker, a former bank robber on heroin. Or maybe a senior who had dementia might have wandered into the room by mistake. Nobody would be turned away.

I had visited some at their homes, met others for coffee, I met their children, and occasionally I had intervened with God's word and prayer when, for instance, a crack addict whose house was upside down telephoned me to ask for a bible. I had worked at VIRCC with some, and I visited others at recovery centers, helped one or two with their rent and had supported two in court and at VIRCC and William Head Institution parole hearings. Of course, this support that I gave was through my faith in Jesus Christ. The most painful court hearing to me, was a "child custody battle".

A young man who brought his bible and guitar to our two meetings was always a sight for sore eyes. He was almost always so cheerful. He played his guitar and sang at the end of our Connection to Freedom meeting at both the Mustard Seed and the Salvation Army. It was Friday night and our meeting at the Salvation Army had come to an end. We were outside, talking about the message I had given. Last week I thanked the young man with the bible, and guitar, for the song he gave us at the end of the meeting. I said, "Good night, see you next Friday!" to a few stragglers.

On the way home I remembered my commitment for the coming week, to speak with three different schools: Parkland, Claremont and a Camosun College Criminal Justice Program class. I was looking forward to sharing with the students and I felt happy and content, and as I settled on my couch, I thanked the Lord. A half hour later, maybe an hour, I answered the ringing of my telephone.

By the close of that weekend, I had received calls from: Delta, Victoria, and Vancouver police, and news radio reporters. I had given a requested interview to Chek Six television. It appeared our young bible reading, guitar player, had gone "missing". A call from his sister made that clear to me. I learned about the youth's family and their love for him which was without question.

At each of my school speaking engagements, from Monday on, I talked about our young man and how he was presumed "missing". Each teacher granted me permission to post his picture that I'd had blown up by an office supply company. By phone I reached out to churches and community concerns that he might have frequented. My concern had become my attitude of prayer that our 26-year-old Connection to Freedom member, would be found.

Days seemed like weeks as I waited to hear something, as we all waited for news. Following our Friday night meeting at the Salvation Army, he had taken the Victoria to Vancouver ferry intent to visit his parents. That's all I knew for sure! The next TV News shocked me to the core! The news was that Delta Police, near the Tsawwassen Ferry Terminal, had found a dead body.

I received phone calls from the young man's mother, expressing a desire to come to Victoria to attend a Connection to Freedom meeting to say thanks for the support we had given her son.

She and her daughter, his sister, arrived in Victoria and telephoned me. That night they came to our Connection to Freedom meeting that we were holding at the Mustard Seed. About 8 or 9 members and I sat listening in our Connection to Freedom meeting. The mother, and sister, revealed how the young man had committed suicide, by drowning himself. "Why?" we asked, shocked to hear this. The mother's reply was "Mental illness!" I was riveted to my seat! "He had the type of sickness that could not easily be detected!" The sister continued: "Because for the most part, his behavior was viewed as being normal".

I have over several years, on-line, viewed this young man playing his guitar and singing his songs. Often his singing has uplifted me. Not only this but a non-profit organization in his name started by his friends and family on the mainland, has done much toward Mental Illness. - author

Wilkinson Road Jail

I believe my crime had something to do with burglary. I was thinking about my suicide attempt in California, when I was a month shy of my 19th birthday. I would never tell anybody the truth. I'd always say it was "a road accident". At the jail, which was in Saanich, I was about 21 or so. I stood against the bars one day looking down to the main floor. Looking up at me was an inmate who was a drinking buddy from the outside world. He yelled: "Hey, Steve, what's the matter, did you come to jail because all your friends are in here?" I laughed as if I had just heard the funniest joke, at some Comedy show. The reason I thought it so funny is because nobody on earth knew it, but I was sure I would never again come back to jail. These other guys are regulars, they can't help themselves.

Listening to an old con from back east who was the joint barber and I'll never forget his words to me: "I've been in penitentiaries across Canada, but nothing was as bad as this Wilkinson Road Jail!" Somewhere inside of me I felt proud to be associated with "Wilky" as we inmates named the jail in our conversations. Some called it "Wilky Beach". My mind flashed to our early morning work gangs, The Shoemaker Shop, The Tailor Shop, but I was working at the Piggery on the farm. Occasionally some citizen whose friend was on the inside, left a bottle of wine at the farm gate. An inmate would jump from the truck bed to close the gate and would scoop whatever had been left by the well- meaning citizen. After work, we would line up according to our work detail and be frisked by the guards.

There was a time when I worked in the Clothes Change were fresh from the outside, men changed their clothes for jail issue, making them just another inmate of Wilkinson Road Jail. They were either sentenced or awaiting a court hearing or a sentence by the judge.

The Bull Pen prior to changing their clothes, was so medieval looking that "fish" (brand new to the prison system) where sometimes emotionally shaken when they reached me and my co-worker in Clothes Change. There were "tough guys" who wanted the best clothing, but unless they had rewarded me, seldom did I OK their request. For example, on more than one occasion I let a tube of toothpaste through, that had drugs in it. But I got a taste at least after work.

I remembered the Tailor Shop when I was a helper there. That was the not-so-secret tattoo "connection". Three needles melted into the end of a toothbrush, and dipped in India Ink from the Tailor Shop, that was the prize for working there. Deals were to be made there.

One evening an inmate from below my tier called, "Hey, Steve, do you want to join us. We've got a group going and I've been watching you, you seem like you can handle yourself. The other day I saw you punch out that goof on your tier! I'll talk to you after the count (that's when all inmates line up at their cell doors and guards walk down the tiers counting us) Just to make sure that nobody had escaped since the last count or had died.

When I met with the inmate who was wanting me to join his group, it turned out he was asking me to become a gang member for which he was the founder. He referred to other inmates that had tried but failed to measure up to what he was looking for. "That's when I watched you smack that guy on your tier!" I did not recognize who I had become or was becoming, so I replied, "Sure, but who is in the gang, and what do you do?" "We've got a guy on a murder beef, a biker, and we've got a secret handshake! But first you need to get our gang tattoo. But what in this jail do you do?" I asked again. His answer told me that we bully weaker inmates who are goofs, and fish who don't know any better, to steal their canteens.

I was out of tobacco the day I accepted the gang leader's invitation to become one of them. I learned the secret handshake and received the gang tattoo. I noticed one or two other inmates had the same inked symbol. We acknowledged each other. But I was reading a magazine when a shaky inmate was stabbing me with needles melted into a toothbrush end that he kept dipping into a bottle of India Ink. The tattoo he gave me was a very poor "Butterfly" on my left hand. I didn't know why he was so nervous, but his hands shook like an old man's hands.

I had muscled inmates for their canteens, especially chosen by me. Making sure inmates saw my gang tattoo. As far as I know but I could be wrong, the gang came to an end when after his release from jail our leader stole a car and crashed into a concrete wall killing himself.

Lakeview Forestry Camp

With two other guys I was busted on Cook Street while on our way to rob a jewelry store. We were charged with possession of burglary tools. The Wilkinson Road Jail classification officer had shipped me up island, about five hours drive from the jail to Lakeview a Forestry camp near Campbell River. My two pals, the co-accused, were doing their bits on the mainland in Oakalla Prison. They wanted to split us up, I guess. I was feeling as sick as a dog after withdrawal from heroin. The first guard in a white hard hat and uniform that spoke to me said, "I hate convicts!" He was a former Vancouver cop. The first inmate conversation I heard was about an inmate being raped in the bush. This was not a shock to me, because I had seen other "inmates abusing inmates" scenes.

Being forty pounds underweight I could barely climb the camp steps. I needed heroin! The smallest task was a real effort for me. From my hut, (each hut with about ten inmates) to the kitchen, was like I imagined climbing Mount Everest would be when a person is junk sick. Three weeks later and clean and sober by the force of my will, I began to fit in with my fellow inmates and took in an occasional AA meeting. I attended the camp's High School classes, but I failed to graduate. The night the inmates received their certificates of graduation I called out to the schoolteacher: "You couldn't even pass me when I was just a few points short! Some help you are. I wish I'd never tried to do better!

Anything that happens to me from now on is your fault!" As for Chapel, although I was given the opportunity to, as they say, "get religion", I acted contrary to all 'goody two shoes' teachings. In short, I was filled with resentments against anything to do with God for allowing me to suffer. Still, there was a change taking place inside of me that I could not understand.

I worked on the logging crew as a chaser on the landing. But I was injured when a rain slicked log pinned me between other logs. So, I got the job in the Camp Laundry. I looked after the whole camp working nights so I could also lift weights in the gym. And I had stashed some smuggled booze behind a washing machine in a non-identifiable container. A jail house brew that had been fermenting for weeks was opened and as RCMP cars sped into the camp, I could see below different groups of inmates fighting. I had no need for a home- made brew because unbeknown to anybody I was sipping on the real thing, whiskey. I received letters from my mom and one from some guy she was living with who I had never met. She sent me a pair of sunglasses which I used in the winter and summer.

The winter was cold, rainy and there was lots of snow, and the summer was blistering heat. A toothache had almost driven me mad but, better late than never, I was driven to the dentist. One winter night I awoke when the inmate responsible for keeping our stoves lit was sticking a red-hot piece of coat hanger in his mouth. This was to cauterize a bleeding gum after he had pulled out his own tooth that was giving him fierce pain for weeks. In the bush brew shacks were built by inmates for their fellow workers. I saw a man take an axe to his own knee so he could be sent back to Wilkinson Road Jail. But all said and done, his self-imposed injury was not bad enough. The problem was he slept in the bunk next to me. Inmates thought he was an undercover RCMP, and they gave him a rough time.

Finishing my nine-month sentence I said my farewells and after receiving a ride to Campbell River I caught the bus to Victoria. Fit and tanned, and to my pre-heroin weight I sat back and, in my thoughts, planned my next steps in Victoria: A fix of heroin, a glass of booze, and a woman. Although the order might change, those were my priorities. After that I would look for work. "The best laid plans of mice and men fall quickly by the wayside", and they sure did!

One year later, I would be fired from a janitorial job, when one of the workers told the boss I had a criminal record. Several weeks later I had my first epileptic seizure.

Two Parolees

"I am on parole living at a Halfway House (for Federal parolees) and I go to the Connection to Freedom group on Thursday nights. It was through Chaplain Steve that I received the opportunity to speak with you in this book: At 13 the police got me for shoplifting and skipping out of school. By 15, I was done with school. I used mescaline, acid, and I was injecting speed. I got established as a dealer on the streets, buying in bulk and selling in bulk. Between 16-17, I was Wanted across Canada. They arrested me. I was using 5 different names (aka) under 7 different bails."

"By 17, I was in the Burwash Provincial Jail. Three inmates tried to take me down and this led to me escaping. I got caught and given 4 more years. I was put in Workworth Prison for a couple of years. Collins Bay came next. Then over the next 10 years I made the prison circuit in every penitentiary in the area. I am 57 years old and have spent most of my life in prison. Not because anybody else was to blame. It was the choice I made, and I was prepared to live with the consequences. I just didn't care. When I came to the end of myself, I didn't know how to change. I didn't even know what the word 'self-esteem' meant. I took different programs but today I believe I am the person God intended me to be. Not the person I chose to be." By L

I was totally aware that the parolee I met for coffee and sometimes breakfast had robbed a couple of banks and of course, had paid the price of almost 20 years in prison. I was no stranger to crime and jail myself before Christ's intervention in my life. But as the facilitator of regular weekly group meetings of Connection to Freedom, I had been asked by this man's parole officer to help him with his addiction to heroin, on which I had spent many years myself. But something troubled me at one of our 'morning get togethers'. Something I couldn't put my finger on. The parolee kept interrupting me during our conversation, with outbursts such as "I may as well rob a bank! Society doesn't care about me!" I had never seen him so forlorn, and he kept looking through the window as if expecting someone.

It came to me over the next few days, how to help the troubled man. God had given me this process when I was a VIRCC inmate. The Connection to Freedom book. It was not about shaming the book participant; it was about adults helping youth at risk through their stories. I suggested the parolee, help school students and youth groups, with his story. It was his recommendation that I write his story while he goes through heroin withdrawal. Whether the parolee used that as an excuse to use heroin or he planned to use it anyway, I don't know. But during his withdrawal, I learned that he was a Christian and had been baptized at an Easter church service.

Next, I learned he was in a Recovery Centre on the mainland, where I visited him. He was no longer a parolee. But he had attended Connection to Freedom meetings in Victoria and perhaps something was said that sparked his desire to change his life. The one thing I knew for sure is that he and I had prayed together often and shared scripture with one another and that twice we had told our stories to Camosun College Criminal Justice students. I believe he had put his bank robbing days behind him.

Steroids, my nightmare!

I am on Probation, living in a recovery house. I was just released from Vancouver Island Regional Correctional Centre. I am giving my story to Steve of the "Connection to Freedom" group in hope of getting my message out to young people about the abuse of steroids and the consequences that I live with every day of my life. Steve is writing and I'm telling him my story.

I started weight training in my twenties and was very competitive in sports. It was about this time I saw a picture of a bodybuilder, and I knew I wanted to be just like him. I was willing to get there no matter what the cost. My first experiment with steroids was through a doctor I knew who would hand out anything I wanted. Why steroids? I was told by a world-famous body builder that if I wanted to compete, I would have to go on steroids. That was mistake number one. Not having the doctor do any blood work or follow up examination was foolish. That was mistake number two.

By 1986 I was living in Vancouver and worked as a door man at a night club. Now at 240 pounds of muscle and a mind twisted by steroids, I did what I wanted in a life filled with sex, drugs and rock 'n' roll. For six months all I did was work out, shoot steroids, drink, do drugs, and try to control the rage that was beginning to boil inside of me, and I moved with my then girlfriend down to California.

Ending up in Palm Springs I soon established myself at a gym in Palm Desert. Here I found out the easiest and cheapest way to get steroids was to travel to Mexico where I gave the pharmacist my list and it was filled with no problem. All I had to do now was smuggle the steroids back across the border. When entering Mexico I would use my Canadian ID and when I returned, I would use my American ID.

Instead of doing six-week cycles and weaning off the steroids for a period, I increased the different types I used as well as the amount I used was way over the recommended doses. As a matter of fact, I never knew the right doses and never cared about it anyway. Why worry? Nothing could hurt me, ever! In my twisted thoughts I was a Superman on top of the world.

I trained six days a week and would grow very depressed if I missed my workout and my moods were changing drastically. My personal relationship with my girlfriend was suffering as well as my work. I began to hang around with the wrong kind of people. I craved the adrenaline rushes and became bored with the "ordinary" whatever that was. Now all that mattered was training, using steroids and getting bigger. I had another problem too. How was I going to control all the rage and my uncontrollable urge to strike out at anything?

I was tying the laces of my running shoes one day and one of my laces snapped and so did I. The steroid rage was now here, uncontrollable, quick, and violent. All I could see was 'red'. I was now a 260-pound monster with no conscience whatsoever when enraged. I trashed my house with the authority of a raging bull in a China shop.

As the years went on, my attitude and my emotions grew more unstable until one day I found myself all alone and filled with anger. Now the street gang years started. This led to methamphetamine use. Now with crystal meth, steroids and alcohol, all hell was about to break loose. In the street gang which was in Southern California I was a menace to society, and I loved every minute of it. With a combination of guns, steroids, and crystal methamphetamine, even my own gang members were terrified of me. Eventually with two bullet holes in me and a few broken bones I was jailed for a very large robbery.

After doing my time in one of the most violent atmospheres you can imagine I was released into the hands of the INS (Immigration and Naturalization Services) and shipped down to Calexico, a Federal prison on the Mexico/US border. Finally released in 1994 I was put on a plane to Vancouver with only the clothes on my back and sixteen dollars in my pocket.

Sitting at the Vancouver Airport with nowhere to go I telephoned an old girlfriend who brought me some food and clothes. I was headed for my sister's house in another part of the country.

Now back in Canada I was still using steroids, dealing drugs and I got very careless! One night when I was injecting Testosterone into my thigh muscle I heard a knock at the door. My friend had shown up and wanted to "party" and find another girlfriend for the night. I quickly threw the syringe into the fridge and not giving it a second thought I went out for a Friday night of fun. The next day, groggy from the night before, I used the syringe from the fridge without cleaning it up. One month later I lay in the hospital emergency room unable to move. My family was called in because I was not expected to make it through the night.

Everywhere the steroids had weakened my bone structure infection attacked. After six weeks I was released. But it was not over! Unknown to anyone the infection raged on and ate my right hip joint away before they could stop it. My first operation and lots of steel later, my hip was fused, and I wore a body cast for seven and a half months. For the next six months I was homebound with intravenous antibiotics running through my veins every four hours.

The fight for my life was still on. This was a nightmare I was not prepared for. After six weeks and my veins now gone, I graduated to oral antibiotics. I still trained after this even in my body cast and by using crutches. At this time CBC Television followed me around as they were doing a documentary on steroids.

Five years later I had my first hip replacement. Pain and the pain killer morphine went hand in hand together. The hip replacement did not take. The steel rod that went down into my leg bone was now loose and sliding from side to side. The movement would bring me to tears. So, they gave me a larger dose of morphine which kept me going in my own little world.

Today I still have problems with my hip and my left knee is starting to break down due to my long-term ABUSE OF STEROIDS. My knee will soon have to be replaced. I am determined to go on and tell others, anywhere in the world who will listen to my misadventures so they won't be tempted to say, as I did, "Nothing can harm me. I'm Superman!" But if I was such a big deal, why did I also end up in County Jails at Riverside, Indio, Blythe, and San-Diego, California?"

I went to the "Connection to Freedom" meetings for five years and I was a member of their Board of Directors and for six years I was a co-speaker with Steve Bradley at the Parklands Senior Secondary and other high schools.

I love the Lord and one of my scripture favorites is Matthew 6:33.

'G' died a relatively young man. It turned out he was ex-US Military. Therefore the US flag was partially draped over his place of rest. He served as an employee of Salvation Army ARC in Victoria, BC.

"My opioid blackout!"

In 1986 I visited a girl I knew well from the street. She was a kind-hearted and streetwise person. We both knew the streets well, but the saddest part of her life was that she had a gaping hole in her arm caused by an infection from shooting cocaine with a dirty needle. We drank some wine and popped some pills. I didn't know it then, but I would one day be diagnosed with Hep C, from shooting heroin in jail with a dirty needle. Suddenly that day I found myself standing in front of a Douglas Street pharmacy. I became blind with anger. But why? The focus of my rage was a pharmacist. I had nothing against the man and didn't try to rob him of drugs. Although homeless, my crime was not for money either. That man just happened to be at the wrong place at the wrong time. At that moment I was lashing out at the world to make someone pay for the bad cards that I felt life had dealt me.

With a sudden desire to strangle this gray-haired druggist, I crept behind him and began to place my hands around his throat. But then the strangest thing happened! Some force in the shadowy form of my stepdad intervened! This shock changed my feelings from revenge to compassion and I gave up my strong-armed action. As if he were a guardian, a customer entered the picture to aid the druggist. With a sigh of relief that I had not strangled the man, I gave no struggle but waited for the police. When I snapped out of my addict blackout, I was looking at the faces of some Victoria policemen. I managed to say, "Take me to Wilkinson Road Jail!" I felt the familiar cold steel of handcuffs clasp my wrists. Looking at life from the inside of a police wagon once again, I felt confused, lonely and without hope.

Next morning, I woke up in a cell at the Victoria Police Station. I spent many nights there when I was a kid. Usually, it was for bar fights and related mischief. My head was pounding, and I felt deathly sick. I would have given anything for a drink of booze or a needle-full of heroin. Just then a jailer called out, "Bradley, do you want to read the newspaper? You've made the headlines this time!" I had no idea why I was in a police cell nor what the meaning was behind his words. That morning in April

1986, I went to court to hear my charges. I was stunned when I heard the judge say, "Attempted robbery!" Fortunately, the John Howard Society of Victoria, an offender and ex-offender organization, bailed me out. I had been a client of theirs for many years.

The judge stipulated that I go for Alcohol and Drug Abuse counselling, attend NA meetings and report in person three times a week to a bail supervisor. Since I was homeless and living on welfare, I had been couch-surfing. And occasionally I curled up on the dirty floor of a Fort Street flophouse. The first thing I had to do was find a place to live. So, after listening to the judge give his instructions to me, I signed some documents then went to the John Howard Society. They were helpful but, even after trying everything, the organization couldn't find a place for me to live. So, leaving their View Street office, I headed to the Liquor Store.

With a bottle of whiskey tucked into my jacket, I walked about two or three miles it seemed, to Beacon Hill Park where I proceeded to get drunk. After a couple of hours, I staggered to a friend's house. He and I put our heads together and by the end of the day we came up with some oxycodone and a bottle. Behind my actions was a sense of sheer hopelessness and a crazed desire to kill myself. So, I drank myself into oblivion while shoving pills into my mouth. This suicidal behavior was routine for me and waking up in the Royal Jubilee Hospital, I was told how doctors had saved my life. An overdose of alcohol mixed with opioids, had almost ended my life but for a man walking his dog who called an ambulance.

It came time for me to go for my drug and alcohol counselling, a three-month program called "The Abstinence Group". The only problem being I was in a bed at the Royal Jubilee Hospital with paddle marks on my chest. My heart had stopped from an overdose of opioids and alcohol and doctors had brought me back to life. But I was not happy or thankful. Like my other suicide attempts, I had failed! But why was I so bent on killing myself?

A picture in my mind of when I was kidnapped and abused, at 17, near Stave Lake, BC, had never revealed itself to me, to Psych Ward psychiatrists, or to Alcohol and Drug counselors, because as the human mind will do for self-preservation, the tragic event was so severe that my mind had blocked my memories of that time. But whether I was aware or not, experiencing the deep pain of that abuse was so horrendous, that even alcohol and heroin were not sufficient to give me relief. Suicide, although I fought against it, seemed my only answer.

Only God Himself could see that my jail term related to this drug store madness, would be a blessing for me and would result in the founding of the Connection to Freedom meetings, and Connection to Freedom book (with Janet's help). But first I would have to call on the name of Jesus Christ.

A Blessing in Jail

The date today is August 11, 2024. The Lord has blessed me since August 29th, 1987, and I have joy in my heart that He has continued helping me to "Help these men" as was His call on my life in cell 15, Living Unit D, Vancouver Island Regional Correctional Centre, Saanich, BC, Canada. Allow me to encourage you with this shared blessing.

He was a violent man and was well known for his violence, and problems he caused. I was remembering this as I walked toward the unit he was in. I had seen him arrive at the Vancouver Island Regional Correctional Centre in leg irons. He had been flown by plane to Victoria from what he called, "a big penitentiary in California." He had asked to see me.

So, believing it was probably some kind of request for me to let him know which inmates had drugs, or some other scam, before I left my unit to meet with the guy, the violent inmate, I had prayed to the Lord. I wondered whether I should take a Bible with me. But it didn't seem the Lord's will, so I was sitting in a chair next to the inmate who was lying on his bunk.

He told me the reason why he had asked to see me was because he heard I had become a Christian. He thanked me for coming to see him. I listened as he spoke: "Those penitentiaries in California are about survival. The prison I was at is a tough joint. Every day you must survive. There's only one way I've found" (as he raised a Holy Bible that had obviously 'been through the wars'). I was beyond amazed! Truly, I would have stayed there all day if I could have.

This inmate who had caused problems for the BC correctional system, showed me God at work. He shared with me how his younger brother who is also at VIRCC had told him about Connection to Freedom.

The inmate who had been taken from his California penitentiary, asked me to take his Bible to his younger brother. When I handed the Holy Bible, to his brother, he had tears in his eyes. There was nothing phony or a con game, about this, a blessed experience from the Lord, for which I say, Praise God! - author

I say then: Walk in the Spirit, and you shall not fulfill the lust of the flesh. Galatians 5:16

Prayer is powerful

Among the biggest blessings I received is when, first as a friend, then as a chaplain, I visited a former sex trade worker with Aids, who was dying, then a former Connection to Freedom group member, an alcoholic, who from alcohol, was dying, and third, a former employee of the Mustard Seed Food Bank, who because of cigarettes, was dying. Their last moments in all cases, not only because of medication, but there was an unbelievable, if I might say, "joy" even "peace" in each person that I witnessed. A fourth and fifth person whom I visited with were, well, you'll see as you read. There came the day when I invited Dr. Jack formerly a physician, who had attended our Connection to Freedom meeting, for three years, to join me.

An elder with the Oak Bay Gospel Assembly, was at the Royal Jubilee Hospital, and was dying. Dr Jack and I listened as Roy, the elder, keeping a brave face, smiled but quickly lost any semblance of happiness probably because of his pain. Dr. Jack and I, did all we could to uplift his spirits but although Roy tried, he tired easily and it was time for us to leave. Prayers for him seemed like our last offering before saying our good by's. Suddenly the Holy Spirit led me to ask Roy to pray for Dr. Jack and I, instead.

The elder who had regularly supported Connection to Freedom, gave out a joyous "yell" so loud that nurses walking the corridor turned around, "Praise the name of Jesus! I'm still of use to you Lord!!!" He then prayed over us and as he did, I remembered his message one night when he visited us at the Needle Exchange. Kurt had actually counted and there were 51 people: addicts, ex-offenders, people of the street, drawn to our Connection to Freedom meeting. The elder went to be with the Lord not long after our visit with him. But even today in my spirit I can still see him smiling.

At the same hospital but much later, with a member of our Board, I visited an addict I had known for many years. But in the hospital because of his pain, he was high on Dilaudid. My only words were "I see you've got some good drugs in you now" and he gave a half laugh, and the Board member did also. The patient, my old friend, was not a believer in Christ and when it was time for the Board member and I to leave, he didn't want the prayers I offered. But I had brought with me a copy of my book, "Christ's healing touch for addictions", Foreword by Dr. Douglas Hamm, and I asked him if I could leave it as I placed the book on the night stand beside his bed. His comment, in a gruff and inebriated voice, "You know I'm not religious Steve, but I might take a look at it!" That evening my old friend, and co-drug user with me, many years prior, died.

The Victoria General Hospital was my next visit. A young woman who was dying because of domestic abuse, was on life support. No sooner had I caught sight of her when although I tried to walk into her hospital room, because we were such close friends, I could not continue only to be met by the machine that was keeping her alive. However, I attended her funeral and swore to God that I would make sure her death was not in vain.

That month as a guest of Parkland Secondary School, I spoke about my friend who had died from abuse, both domestic and street violence, and wrote her first name on the blackboard. While asking the students if anyone in the class was being abused, at home or otherwise. After class one female student talked with me about the abuse she was receiving at home. I listened, knowing my friend, did not die in vain, and left the troubled student my e-mail address. Since, I have prayed many times for that young student.

"Thank you to the Churches!"

One morning before setting out to Pandora Avenue with my Bible in hand and 50 business cards in my pocket announcing our "Connection to Freedom" meetings, I prayed. That morning, I felt moved to write a letter to a church on Walker Street in Oklahoma City. I had earlier sent my words of encouragement with a silent prayer for the recipients. It was 1995 and the tragedy of the Oklahoma City bombing was being shown on every TV newscast in Canada, the United States and, indeed, globally.

In the early days of my "Connection to Freedom" meetings and counselling, the Mustard Seed Street Church lent me space in their outreach and a room for counselling with parolees, and addicts. And I was invited to serve on their Board of Directors, then called the Church Council. Also, at the invitation of the Victoria Rotary Club, through the Mustard Seed's Senior Pastor Tom Oshiro who was a member, I shared my experiences with Rotarians on two occasions. I was asked to help to acquire funding for the Hope Farm. So, I was more than happy to speak about God, addiction, and recovery.

For some 20 years I was a member of the Mustard Seed Street Church which held services on Sunday afternoons. For several years, however, before going to church, I held "Connection to Freedom" meetings borrowing space from Centennial United Church. Their Board of Directors also loaned me a room to present my counselling sessions. I recall that for eight months a homeless man dragged himself through all kinds of weather from the bush where he lived to attend our "Connection to Freedom" meeting every Sunday morning. Through a group member, who was our occasional piano player, the homeless man eventually found a home.

Three of our several years at Centennial United Church were very special to me in view of my connection to California as a youth. Motivated by the sorrow of "9/11" that I felt for the United States, we as a group bought a small U.S. flag and pinned it to our meeting room wall. In my introduction to our Sunday morning "Connection to Freedom" meeting, I reminded our group that we must pray for hope and for the healing of all those in the United States who were "9/11" victims, including the survivors, their families and the first responders. And we also prayed for the state of New York. Our group took a collection for the victims and families affected by the earthquake in Haiti, Hurricane Katrina in the United States, and the devastating Storm Sandy were in our prayers as well. But, just as importantly, we prayed during these times for God's protection and healing for those communities.

Reacting to school shootings and other tragedies or just because the Lord happened to place them in my heart, with the Holy Spirit inspiring me, I wrote prayer poems leading me to ask our group to pray for healing from tragedies in Canada, the U.S., and the United Kingdom. We prayed in "Connection to Freedom" meetings for God to bless each place according to their needs. He moved me through our group prayers, and I reached out to Central Baptist Church to present a workshop using my workbook and the Bible. I helped with their Saturday morning street breakfasts. Following each meal, which was co-presented by the Glad Tidings Pentecostal Church, I went to a room provided for my "Connection to Freedom" Bible Study support group for people of the street, and others.

The people from the street numbered only ten initially and fewer came each week. Finally, after the last remaining person stopped attending our group, I left the church feeling as if I had failed. But this was only my bruised ego. I stopped at the doorway to see a beautiful sight. Church members were kneeling in front of some street folks washing their feet gently and with compassion. Blistered, cracked, and bruised feet were being cared for. I was in awe at such a selfless act as I looked on to see the joy this gave to the street folk and church members alike. I felt a little ashamed of my self-pity at the end of my workshop.

A very special event for me occurred at Emmanuel Baptist Church when I came face to face with the druggist I had assaulted many years earlier during my attempted robbery of his drug store. This church had invited me to share my testimony and that day following the service, after 14 years of my refusing to ask the druggist's forgiveness for my 1986 crime, the Lord brought me face to face with him. He only said, "I'm glad you didn't kill me!" I was speechless! He was the druggist I had assaulted! But God has a purpose for everything. After a year out on bail which, to be honest, allowed me to shoot heroin and pop opioid pills like oxycodone, my crime resulted in an 18-month term at the Vancouver Island Regional

Correctional Centre where I went through cold-turkey withdrawals. It was the blackest time of my life. But in my jail cell that was the time my life was transformed by Jesus Christ.

The druggist, whose name was John, and I, knew that day when I shared my testimony, as did some members of the church, that a miracle had occurred. I had no way of knowing the druggist was a member of the Emmanuel Baptist Church. He and I were both smiling when we hugged each other. Through the power of the Holy Spirit, God's forgiveness had taken place. Kurt, my co-worker who had joined me that day to hand out our "Connection to Freedom" flyers and business cards, was also smiling. Dr. Doug and Jane, dear friends, and supporters, gave me support that day, confirming God's miracle.

Sometime later Centennial United Church invited me to speak at their Sunday Service. Prayerfully, I gave God's message about the power of forgiveness. Following my talk, a man approached me with tears in his eyes and I will never forget the blessing in what he said: "I am a commercial pilot. I come from Seattle. Now I know why the Lord brought me here. I needed to hear what you had to say about forgiveness (Mark 11:25-26). Thank you and God bless you."

Centennial United Church also hosted our "Connection to Freedom" benefit concert to which we had invited churches to come and give their messages. Also, some musicians donated their time and Centennial United Church members provided tables of food. It was a sincere blessing for everyone. But the one thing above all others that stands out for me was a man I saw in the doorway. He had given his life to the Lord when he was an inmate by reading a Bible and feeling moved by the Holy Spirit. He had been a part of our weekly "Connection to Freedom" meeting for addicts at the Vancouver Island Regional Correctional Centre. The Chaplains advertised our meeting as a "Christian recovery group for inmates with addictions". The next page is for you to write your testimony in Christ. This is an opportunity to glorify the Lord in all that you have learned about Him, through this Workbook. Sharing your testimony (in writing, and verbally) is reaching out to others who are suffering because they don't know Jesus Christ.

'My Testimony in Christ' Exercise

"And they overcame him by the blood of the Lamb
and by the word of their testimony…"

Revelation 12:11

Name...

Date...................................

_____
_____
_____
_____
_____
_____
_____
_____
_____
_____
_____
_____
_____
_____
_____
_____
_____
_____
_____
_____
_____
_____
_____

"Prayers for Duncan, BC, Church"

As in his testimony in this workbook, Pastor Aneil may have travelled to Las Vegas in his drug fueled journeys and attended rehab in California but when the Lord Jesus Christ called him, Duncan, BC, was the most important place on earth. It was there that a God given fellowship joined forces with him and through many who put their hands to the plough, Connection to Freedom Community Church was born.

Note: Should you wish to send an e-mail to Pastor Aneil. aniel.per@gmail.com

To send a letter to him by mail,
Connection to Freedom Community Church
#1 -5201 Trans Canada Highway
Duncan, BC, V9L 6W3

"Prayers for Quesnel, BC, Churches"

I was talking with Reima-Lee, my friend who is a social worker who had come to visit me. We are very close friends; in fact, she saved my life in 2010 when I almost had a nervous breakdown. She was a member of the Connection to Freedom meetings and had served on our board of directors. As we sat reliving some past experiences in ministry, Reima Lee told me her story, which was amazing!

"I was homeless back in 2002. I had slept on a park bench and woke up shivering cold. The night before, I had seen a light and an open door of a rundown motel. There, a lady motioned to me to "sleep on the cot tonight" and then tomorrow I'd go to sleep at the homeless shelter, hungry, addicted to alcohol and drugs, and without hope.

Fast-forward to 2024 and I am alcohol and drug free with degrees in social work including training in Indigenous rights.

"Steve, going to Connection to Freedom meetings saved my life. The reason I went to the meeting is because you, group leader, were once a heroin addict, and you had been homeless like me. Your bible counseling in that room at Centennial United Church helped me. You had become a Chaplain through Mustard Seed Street Church".

Reima Lee and I discussed churches. I was happy she had come down from the Williams Lake area and had attended the Connection to Freedom Community Church in Duncan, BC, that is shepherded by Pastor Aneil a dear friend of mine.

Reima-Lee said, "My journey has only just begun. Please pray for Cariboo House Church, North Star Church, and Cheryl of 'The Way' ministry.

Note: Cariboo House Church, North Star Church, and Cheryl of 'The Way' Ministry, are in my prayers, and our prayers. God's blessing to each one, and all of you.

"Prayers for a Texas Church"

My friend, Dr. Doug, and I, were invited by Aneil, my successor, since my 2013 retirement, to speak at the Connection to Freedom meeting. I was invited on three different occasions to share my testimony and God's word. At the end of each presentation, whatever was the greatest need in my heart, I asked for prayers from the group audience. The heaviest weight was the opioid crisis, but what couldn't leave my mind was the need for prayers for healing for the church and community in Sutherland Springs, Texas.

I thought back to November 5th, 2017, when the television newscasts showed scenes from Sutherland Springs, a small town in Texas that was overshadowed by evil in the form of a killer's rampage. According to media, 26 members of their First Baptist Church were dead, and another 20, had been wounded as they worshipped God that morning.

When asked by some TV reporters about their needs, community members and first responders alike made "prayers for Sutherland Springs" a priority. TV interviews about this senseless mayhem were seen all over the world on international news networks.

I prayed for God's healing for this community of about 600 people. And for the pastor and his wife who lost their daughter to the madness of the shooter. I prayed for families and first responders who have had to cope with this devastating tragedy. I pray for the First Baptist Church in Sutherland Springs, Texas.

Note: An update is that every year since the massacre a "sacred ceremony" is held called "Ringing the Bell" which is in memory of those who lost their lives in what is called one of the worst mass shootings that Texas has ever suffered. I encourage you to remember this church in your prayers in 2024, and in the future.

Prayer Poems

Three of our several years at Centennial United Church were very special to me, given my connection to California as a youth. Motivated by the sorrow of 9/11 that I felt for the United States, we as a group bought a small US flag and pinned it to our meeting room wall. In my introduction to our morning Connection to Freedom meeting, I reminded our group that we must pray for hope and for the healing of all those in the United States who were 9/11 victims, including the survivors, their families and the first responders. And we also prayed for the state of New York.

Through social media, my friend, formerly with the newspaper 'The Bakersfield Californian' sent me his thanks for our prayers for the 9/11 remembrance of 2021. On September 11, 2022, I will be praying, but this time with the addition of how the people of Gander, Newfoundland, Canada, helped an unbelievable number of airplane passengers from the USA during 9/11.

From 1989 to 2023, God inspired me to write the "Prayer Poems" with footnotes. Perhaps you will see "you" in one of the poems, or footnotes, someone you know, a friend, or a family member, and "you too" will be inspired to pray.

– Steve

Song of Hope

Hope is the answer when all else fails
It can't be tasted or seen, only wasted
Cling to hope even with your fingernails
When life has you beaten and pasted

When your grief seems beyond it all
Even if you live far in a distant nation
You'll find friends who'll stand tall
Hope is no one-night infatuation

Hope is the answer when all else fails
It can't be tasted or seen, only wasted
Cling to hope even with your fingernails
When life has you beaten and pasted

This poem is page 106 in my 2015 published work 'Bright Lights in Poems', (thanks Michael Farrell, actor, and director, and my friend, for your encouragement). I wrote this book while recovering from a heart attack. Revisiting the book in 2022, more than at any other time, I saw God's hand in the verses.

Montreal '89

There were 14 students all unaware
Whose minds were on schooling
To assure you that life is still fair
In these words, come our ruling

A tragedy, so bad, is hard to recall
But to forget would only be unfair
Who can we blame if others fall?
And for their families, we still care

The EP was so violent it is true
We will not forget that 6th of December
Our hearts are reaching out to you
In my life and work, we will remember

Since the shootings at Montreal Ecole Technique in 1989, to never forget the fourteen young women who perished, their friends, and their families, I wrote this poem in the early nineties.

Davis Inlet, Labrador

The poor Innu children suffer so much
Youths at Davis Inlet exist without any hope
Gas-sniffing addictions are their ugly crutch
They are suicidal and have no way to cope

In my youth book, I wrote about the plague
Of apathy, desperation, hopelessness
There was no time in 2005 to be vague
Young lives were trapped in dire distress

A friend from Oka, Quebec asked for aid
But I spoke with an audience to blank stares
I left feeling rejected and very much afraid
Surely, someone on this planet must care

My heart aches for all those at Davis Inlet
And I am reminded of the talk I once gave
I write now in righteous anger, and I fret
I pray youths at the Inlet will be saved

In the mid-nineties, I received a letter from a friend in Oka, Quebec. She was very concerned about the Innu children and youths who were sniffing gas and glue at Davis Inlet. I spoke at a church to only blank faces, so I published this poem in two of my books to try and help the Innu. I told their story to high school students.

Road Dancer

The answer was not there out in the field
Or on winding roads that only mystified
So cold and heavy, only evil appealed
Once she skipped rope, so wide-eyed

The years and the pain, no truth to yell
Denial and hate shockingly explode!
Another story for some writer to tell
A lone dancer's life down the road

Tears stain memories of lives in grief
"Who will remind them of our pain?"
A cry in the dark gives some relief
Through the driving snow and rain

If only a white line could but breathe
A simple, straightforward answer
But as hope and courage begin to leave
A car stops and picks up a road dancer

Try not to despair but hold on to hope
Families and friends of loved ones lost
Your pain God sees, He will help you cope
Though your emotions be turned and tossed

I wrote this poem over several years. I thought of BC's 'Highway of Tears', the women lost, their families and friends, and Canada's missing and murdered women. I recognized the great need for prayers. Won't you join me in prayer?

My "Life" Savers

Three times in my life I have been saved
By some First Nations friends of mine
How close was I to being shaved?
I will tell you through these rhymes

Alberta and BC were their homes
On two different Reservations
In the snow and rain, my groans
They gave me their invitations

I was kidnapped and abused
Ten years later in blinding snow
Of sanity, I could not be accused,
And for many years I let no one know

At sixty-four, I had a breakdown
My life was saved by a First Nations friend
She gave me a smile where once was a frown
Because of an e-mail that she did send

I wrote this poem at 7:30 a.m. on July 7, 2022. Through my prayers,
I remembered that I needed to thank some First Nations friends. The
last mentioned was a friend and social worker who had served on our
board of directors.

Again, the Pain!

Bullets fly, losses mount, too raw to speak
Broken people in the shadows of night
Their answers, once again they will seek
Hope sits alone in a candle's light

The innocence in all their young years
Why must such pain, and grief, repeat?
Too many times and too many tears
Their broken hearts, in empty streets

The empty homes, with lonesome pleas
They all did naught to gain such pain
But somehow, on our bended knees
We must remember them, yet again!

When the massacre at a Texas elementary school took young lives, and after I prayed and considered the pain behind the tragedy, by June 24, 2022, this poem was the result. We need to pray for the victims, their families, and their community of Uvalde.

Jack Russell

My brother had a great dog, that's no doubt
He took his Jack Russell many trucking miles
To call his dog my brother would never shout
Yelling was not in my brother's style

He travelled from BC to Washington State
Year after year, and to other US places
When the dog was unwell, he would wait
Until the animal could make paces

Inseparable were my brother and his pet
In the cab of the truck, both were at peace
But a sad moment that I'll not forget
When my brother, in tears, had to cease

It happened one day out of the blue
The Jack Russell died, while on a run
My brother said he didn't have a clue
He buried his dog under the brilliant sun

Words were said over his pet's place of rest
Love poured out through broken hearts
I knew my brother had done his best
And he knew he and his dog had to part

My brother, a long-haul trucker, loved his Jack Russell terrier. He hardly went anywhere without his "friend." In fact, although his site is not active, his profile was a picture of him and his beloved dog. This poem I wrote in the early summer of 2022. My brother now has severe dementia and remembers nothing. His story is in the next poem. Let us pray for all those with dementia.

"Trucker"

He telephoned me from New Jersey,
Texas, Florida and then New York
I felt that he sounded quite 'nervy'
He talked of ham, eggs, and pork

Ohio, New Mexico, then from DC,
He was seeing the world in his truck
His calls were often a comfort to me,
Especially when down on my luck

Blythe, LA, Tupelo and Kentucky
His world was a box on wheels
I thought he was quite lucky
He talked about some crazy deals

California next, then through Ohio,
A stifling desert, then New Jersey
I thought of where else he would go
Suddenly I felt so very unworthy

I'd reached out to him with the cure
I've spoken of recovery and my work
But my love was absent; I am sure
I felt so much like an arrogant jerk

In early 2024 my brother passed away
He had been a trucker for many years
I think of the times, and of his play
And the illness 'dementia' and its fears

My brother and I were close except when ignorantly, I expected him to be perfect. Forgive me brother, and may you rest in peace. Sorry for your loss: to "his family".

"When?"

I spent my youth in the USA
Civil Rights were the worry then
Bad news I heard, again today
Hope seemed to ask, "When?"

Yet another crowd stampedes
Driven by evil and hate
Will the USA ever be freed?
Surely this is not twisted fate

The victims were not to blame
"God, isn't this Your station?"
Or will evil stay, only the same?
Please pray for the whole nation

As a youth in California, it was my privilege to associate with African Americans, Mexicans, and Chicanos, but decades later, has anything really changed? What can make a difference? Jesus Christ, He can help, and He can heal through our prayers of intercession.

My "Jail" Dream

An Empress bids me welcome
As seagulls fill the sky
A causeway made of colors
Attract the passers-by

A suntanned youth in T-shirt
Stands beside a Kabuki Cab
With two girls he starts to flirt
Then he begins to blab

Some grey-haired folks stop
And chat with the young man
On their way to a Tourist Shop
They make their supper plans

When in dreams I entered a door
To walk with these old ghosts
I saw the young ambassador
I lived through this lively host

Then a shadow begins to fall
My heart becomes filled with pain
I'm awakened by a jailer's call,
"Lights out!" once again ...

I was in my cell at VIRCC during a very hot 1987 summer, and visitors with great tans and flashy summer clothing made me wish I wasn't in jail. That night I dreamed my way out.

Cool Hand "fluke"

There was a man of old, locked in chains
Not easily could he crawl or walk
He slugged through winds and bitter rains
He had isolated himself, could not talk

The chains cut deep into his swollen pride
Each step he took was so very hard
In dreams, on an eagle's wing, he'd glide
But then, he turned another card

Three of a kind would set him free
But a stranger's "cold hand" held four
Escape came as he fell to his knees
With trembling hands, he pushed the door

The game of life is but a poker hand
Do you play well? Can you do better?
Twists of fate are not easy to understand
Can you free yourself with plastic or letter?

Inspired by my need to reach out to a gambler who attended our Connection to Freedom meeting at the Salvation Army ARC. The man was struggling with his addiction to the casino and poker, this poem seemed to fit. He always called his winnings "a fluke". I re-published the poem for this present work of 2024.

Love, for one another

There's a headstone in a valley of peace
I visit with my love, my lonely lost, star
Our love is shadows that never cease
No healing inside my emotional scars

I reached for the stars beyond our love
Kept her world to myself, in a dream
When I think of her, I look above
To that light so bright and supreme!

I came alive, with our hope, and joy!
I see her in a wisp of linen green
In her love song, I was her only boy
I was lost to memories now unseen

There's a headstone in a valley of peace
I visit with my love, my lonely lost, star
Our love is shadows that never cease
No healing for me, in my emotions, so far

I wrote this poem on the morning of July 7, 2022, for a friend, whose wife unexpectedly had passed. For several years I had shared my testimony with this friend. He was beginning to ask me questions about spirituality, and the meaning of God. He has since passed. Rest in Peace both of you.

Mother's Day

You were an auburn-haired, bonny lass
With cheeks as pink as the flowers
You have a quick wit, and you have class
Worry has beseeched you for many hours

As I look back now over my life's years
I see extra wrinkles I added to your face
My younger days brought you sad tears
Had I been sober, I'd have felt disgraced

These verses are my true apology to you
I remember your show of upper class
You have helped me make it through
Though in my wild teens, I gave sass

Mom, you have toured the world over
You have seen what is in my dreams
You have walked in fields of clover
You touched Europe's cool streams

So as your hair turns color with time
You sleep a little longer these days
Mom, I love you, not only in rhyme
I love you in so many, many, ways

Thanks to Mark and Teresa who because they provided "Zoom" I was able to tell my mom that I loved her. She passed in 2022, and I miss her a great deal. Readers, how about your moms? Let us pray for all "mothers" on Mother's Day.

Bird's Eye View

Church bells ringing and the lush green grass
The birds brightly sing a song of peace
Dancing together the deer pass
Mainland and Island residents increase

Rivers run silent while others cascade
Beauty shines as springs "give thanks"
Children with pride enjoy the parade
The bagpipes, clowns, and their pranks

People of all races, they soon sorrow
Drive-by shootings, will there be more?
Men and women beg, steal, and borrow
To try and keep the wolf from their door

I walked with my friend along the shores
Vancouver and Victoria are sights to behold
In apathy, yet peace, we give thanks, ask more
Do we help the homeless, their dreams untold?

I finished writing this poem on April 18, 2023. It took me since 2014 to find the right title. But today I recognized the bird's eye view.

"Thank You!"

Before I go let us take one last look
We knew all their lives just like a book
When Connection to Freedom came into your life
It was God's way of healing your heartache and strife

You gave us your heart Janet right from the start
Our book is now finished and soon we will part
You'll soon come to know how famous you are
The Lord has seen fit to make you a star

Please don't be sad that it's come to an end
It's been a real blessing to call you, my friend
When you see this book on somebody's shelf
You'll know it's there because of your inner self

You'll never forget their pain and sorrow
Wherever life leads on your road of tomorrows
What's more, you'll remember what you saw at the end
When darkness threatens, God is your best friend!

It was July 24, 1988, and I was on parole from VIRCC when I wrote this poem. It is Page 224 of the Connection to Freedom book. See Table of Contents for "Janet's Story." As you will learn, the work was hard but a blessing that I thanked God for, daily. Thank you too, Janet.

Prison Circuit

I'm serving time in Washington state
After making the prison circuit
Dealing drugs the reason for my fate
I now say, "It wasn't worth it!"

I was locked up in prison in Minnesota
When I started serving my term
Then I was transferred to Oklahoma
And some good time I earned

I'm trying hard to get an education
I wish in Vancouver I'd stayed in school
Guards here control my every situation
I wish I'd learned the golden rule

I'll send a letter after my appeal
From the Federal Pen I'll call home
When I get out I won't even deal
Drugs only cause my mind to roam

I wrote to this man in Minnesota, Oklahoma, and the state of Washington. But it was his decision to complete his education. I shared Christ with him but at the time he wasn't interested. Still, I remember him and sometimes I will pray for him. That was long ago when I told him about Connection to Freedom meetings and the Connection to Freedom book, that Janet typed.

Garden of Innocence

In a garden made of hope, life had begun
Dreams to be dreamed, worlds to be explored
A gardener sewed seeds under the bright sun
On the horizon, opioid clouds were ignored

So, seeds from the sellers turned to dry rot
Temptations weeds had strangled all hope
Innocence grew, a lowly 'forget me not.'
Enticed into a trap, not one could cope

Acres of gold had turned now to black
Tears soaked the seeds across the land
Gardeners in suits learned of their lack
Delving deeper, they tried to understand

Overseers in rags were burdened much
Miles wide, a question cried, in echoes grand
Why does "innocence" crave a poison's touch?
Planners, once more, strategically they planned

Motivated by a young girl's death from fentanyl, in the spring of 2021, I wrote this poem to tell (a) the history of illicit opioids (b) the addiction, and (c) society's attempts to develop programs. I finished writing it in late summer of 2022. May we all pray for an end to toxic drug deaths, such as illicit fentanyl.

Skid Row Memories

Neon lights shimmer in my darkened gaze
I see a shooting star
The night becomes a shadowed maze
For those who have gone too far

The junkie in his drug-soaked brain
The hooker outside the bar
The wino in his drunken shame
We'd all come way too far

Are you lost in city streets?
Will you "see" any more tomorrow?
I've made another "drug meet"
To hide from all my sorrows

I watch in awe, wonder then pain
At the contents of my rig
Dead friends, in my mind, once again
They too had habits big

I opened my door to a friendly voice
My mind, stoned, was at peace
It was way too late, the wrong choice!
It was the Vancouver City Police...

This was my life, looking through a dirty hotel window on Vancouver's skid row. Years later through Ross the only Christian I knew, I invited Jesus Christ, into my life. But at the point of suicide in my jail cell, ten years later, I re-committed my life to Jesus. Only to find out that He had never forsaken me. The poem on the next page is your opportunity if you want it.

Questions in life

The questions in life are too deep
The weight cripples and prevents sleep
The answers must be in choice, alone
Failing our individuality, we roam

The questions in life are too deep
We give them power, permission to leap
The answers must be in free will, alone
Failing our uniqueness, we roam

The questions in life are too deep
'One day at a time' is a hope to keep!
The answers must be in free speech, alone
Failing our human rights, we roam

The questions in life are too deep
Spirituality, religion, self-will, we weep!
The answers might be in these, alone
Failing our responsibility, we roam

The questions in my life are no more
My search for answers to help the poor
Jesus, I found when near my end
He is closer to me than my best friend

I wrote this poem five years ago as 'addiction recovery' steps. But on the morning of August 18, 2022, I added the last four lines. I completed the poem on March 6, 2023. As I scan over for any mistakes, it is April 9, 2024

"Writing My Poem" Exercise

In the poems you have just read, did anything catch your attention? This exercise is for you to write a poem about, for example, your favorite automobile, your favourite sports activity, your family or your special loved one, your favorite barbecue and picnic, a sunny day when you were a young man or youth. Focus, in your poem not on drugs or alcohol, crime, or prison. If you are a believer in Christ, write a poem about your relationship with Him.

"My Poem"

_____

_____

_____

_____

_____

_____

_____

_____

_____

_____

_____

_____

_____

_____

_____

_____

_____

_____

_____

_____

Drawings

When I was on parole from VIRCC in 1988 and living at the Upper Room (where Our Place is now), one of the places I hung around was the Open Door which was overseen by gentle-spirited Rev. Lawrence. He prayed with me and for me, and for the Connection to Freedom book and meetings. I shot a game of pool there and got to know a couple of street guys and ex-offenders.

Some weeks later a guy moved across from me in the Upper Room and I knew him from the Open Door. I showed him some of my writings and told him of the ministry that God had called me to in jail. He wasn't too interested in God at that time, it seemed. But one day after he saw me reaching out to people on the street, not as a religious fanatic, but in Christ's love, he greeted me with a "hello."

One day my door was open as was his and we just talked about this and that. Suddenly, he asked, "Can you use drawings in your book to help people?" That was it. I knew that God had brought us together. Drawing after drawing over the next three months, he gave me, including a picture of me sitting in the street shelter, the Upper Room, and one of himself as if seen through a keyhole.

As I turned them over to Janet, who was helping me with the book, I asked the street artist if he would like to give me his testimony. He said he'd have to think it over. One morning he said to me, "I've written my testimony if you still want it to help your Connection to Freedom people." When I read about his life experiences, I was pleasantly amazed. The heading was "Connection with the people of freedom" and he wrote:

"The feeling of being alone is worse than anything I have ever known. I attempted to kill my loneliness by using drugs and alcohol for more than half my life, ending up in jails and psychiatric institutions. I have also overdosed a few times and tried to hang myself once. I am thirty-one years old, and this is my testimony through Christ. No matter the way we believe about our faith, if we don't have love, meaning if we cannot give or receive love, then life is like death. 1 Corinthians 13 means so much to me. CONNECTION with the people of FREEDOM has brought me closer to Christ."

I selected one picture from the collection of more than twenty that Glenn had drawn for the Connection to Freedom book.

When Glenn asked me which of the twenty pictures he had drawn for the Connection to Freedom book, did I like? Because the picture reminded me of a man just out of prison whose story I was in the process of writing, I chose this picture. But you would be amazed at Glenn's drawings in the Connection to Freedom book. If ever you want to see those drawings contact Pastor Aneil of Connection to Freedom Community Church because he has access to them. Contact aneil.per@gmail.com

The Birth Place of
1987   Connection to Freedom   1988

Drawn by Janet, who helped with the Connection to Freedom book and attended the Connection to Freedom meetings. The "shining light" above the jail on the left was her way of describing how Jesus Christ entered the heart of a once suicidal inmate, me. Collectively, many inmates were touched by the Lord. Many participated and were helped.

When Billy was an inmate attending Connection to Freedom meetings at VIRCC, as facilitated by Kurt and I, after his release, he continued attending the meetings which were held at the Centennial United Church in Victoria. He was a resident of Duncan, and I visited him several times, and we prayed together. When Billy handed his drawing to me at the jail, he said, "I want to donate my drawing of the Lord, to be used any way you see fit, for the Connection to Freedom program." My co-worker Kurt and I were blessed by this gift. Many Connection to Freedom letters and newsletters over many years carried Billy's drawing as our letterhead.

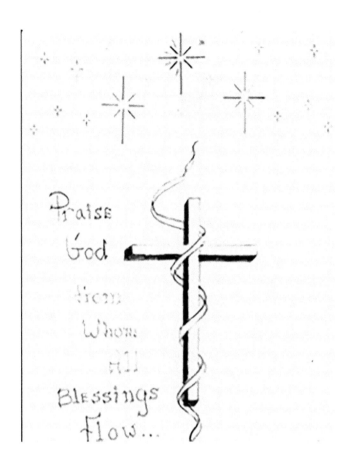

Kerri, who was released from prison in the state of Washington, heard about our Connection to Freedom meetings, and became a regular. Her love of the Lord was easy to see as she became a board member of our Connection to Freedom Jail and Street Outreach Society. During our prayers, Kerri seldom forgot to pray for the women who are in prison, as well as the inmates locally, nationwide and in the USA who were our "pen pals." The drawing was posted in 2021.

I drew this character (me) on Oct 7, 2022, as I reflected on how difficult it was for me after being in jail and then paroled for a year. I could not find any meeting space at the churches for Connection to Freedom meetings. I had shared my testimony in Times-Colonist newspaper, and still nothing, no response at all, even on Chek 6 TV for 8 minutes. No response until the Mustard Seed Board of Directors offered us space which we were glad to accept. Their Board placed me on probation.

"My Drawing" Exercise

Directions: There are several choices, please select one: your favorite animal, your favorite car, your favorite sport. Finally, if God is in your life, a picture of how you see Him, church, or chapel.

"My Drawing"

Rehabilitating offenders

Their motive for committing bank robbery was as different to each man as night is from day. Through our relationship as counselor and counselee, instead of looking for the "war stories", God had me search for and find, "the good" in each of the three men. A fourth man wrote his story and mailed it to me, for the purpose of my school talks.

One day I met with two men separately whose offense was bank robbery. One robbery was in Vancouver and another in Calgary. For which he had served 19 years in different prisons. The second man robbed a bank in Toronto, using a weapon. He had served 17 years in Ontario and BC prisons. And for four years I had corresponded with a federal inmate who had robbed a bank on Vancouver Island.

The first man whose offenses were in Vancouver and Calgary, with his parole officer's permission, accompanied me to Prince George to visit with the inmates at the Prince George Regional Correctional Centre. He also wrote his story for our Connection to Freedom book, and to help "youth at risk". He attended our Connection to Freedom meetings which of course were bible based. Twice he was my co-speaker at Camosun College for the Criminal Justice students.

The second man whose offense was in Toronto, wrote his story and asked me to use it to help the Victoria high school students with whom I spoke frequently. He attended Connection to Freedom meetings and allowed me to interview him for the Connection to Freedom book.

The third man who I had reached out by letter, whose offense was committed on Vancouver Island not only wrote his story for me, "to help youth at risk" but suggested the title for a book I was writing: "The Way It Really Is" which I registered with the National Library of Canada. Twice he was my co-speaker at Camosun College for the Criminal Justice Program students.

The following story sent from prison, is by a man who was there when Connection to Freedom started in Vancouver Island Regional Correctional Centre (VIRCC). But his story was sent from a different prison, two years later.

I gave a man a ride to a Victoria mall and parked in a lot in front of a Trust Company. The man (no name) went inside to cash a cheque. He came out and we left. A few minutes after leaving the Trust Company mall a police car drove by us going the opposite way. The man in the car asked me to keep an eye on the cop car and let him know what was going on. Even though I was high on pills and coming off a 10–12-hour coke run I could still feel the dread enter my body. What had I gotten into?

Two and a half months earlier I had been through a trial for numerous charges laid by the Victoria Police. I was with another guy who had stolen two bags of car stereo equipment. But he got away. I was found guilty; they never caught him, and they held me responsible. At the sight of another police car the man in our car who had just cashed his cheque at the Trust Company, panicked. He told me that he had just robbed the bank, back at the mall. I knew it was either robbery or the cheque he cashed was bogus. For my part I received three years in prison.

In the dope scene, drinking and crime go hand in hand, especially if you need the money to score. In that situation it can be easy to compromise your values and say: "I'm not doing anything, it's the other guy!" The door opens; the police walk in; the dope is on the table; a drink is in your hand. Maybe you don't know about the stolen goods or guns they find. Being there becomes a very important factor in your life, about this time. (I wrote this for the Connection to Freedom book).

The next story is about recovery from addiction, and rehabilitation from criminality:

This story was gained for the Connection to Freedom book program when, at the Upper Room Street shelter, I met this young man. It wasn't long before I invited him to tell me his story, and I asked his OK to include his experiences in the Connection to Freedom book, to help others. As he talked, I wrote. He titled his contribution to the book, "Thumbs Up for Connection to Freedom". His story follows.

At sixteen I spent the night in the Brant County Jail for being a menace and being drunk. I was yelling at some cops and daring them to arrest me. By the time I was seventeen I was in and out of the bucket quite a few times for drinking related offenses. In Brant County Jail I saw a guy slash his wrists with a razor blade and it scared me but not enough I guess because I ended up in the Mimico Correctional Centre in Toronto for Breaking and

Entering. I did this to get money for drugs and alcohol. While I was inside, I lost my girlfriend which is a very common thing when a guy goes to jail.

I started to use speed about that time, and cocaine. I was told by my friends, (so called) that drugs would make me feel better. I did some burglaries when I was twenty years old, and I started fencing hot goods to get money for speed. I was sent to Burtch Correctional Institution when I was twenty-one. Before drugs took control of my life I earned Ribbons, Crests, and Trophies for Hockey, and Soccer and Boxing. I had nine years in Hockey, eight years in Soccer, and I had Boxed for four years and been in Karate for about two and a half years.

I was a real troublemaker when I was sixteen years old. I acted childish and started shoplifting mainly to impress my friends that I could get away with it. I don't think I'm an alcoholic, but I know if I didn't have my book (he was writing a book titled "Thumbs Up!") to occupy my mind, I would probably be doing drugs. Lost and confused standing in front of a mirror reflecting with naive eyes, I see the weakened image of a young man lost in a cruel world.

I am new to Victoria, but I was here no more than a few days when I heard about "The Connection to Freedom book". In my travels around Victoria, I have run into people all over who know about this book. Some of the guys that were in jail at the same time as Steve remember him putting it together. This is a totally amazing time in my life for me because, about four months ago while I was hitching on the Trans-Canada Highway just outside Spanish, Ontario, I was inspired to keep a daily journal. A record if you like, of my daily search for serenity and freedom from drugs and my old habits, meaning "Addiction".

Note: It was 1988 when he told me his story for the Connection to Freedom book. In 2006 he was a co-speaker with me at Claremont Secondary School, and he had hitchhiked 20 or more miles in a heavy downpour, to make it to the school on time. - author

Connection to Freedom Book

Prayerfully I co-ordinated the development and content of the Connection to Freedom book in 1987 while an inmate of the Vancouver Island Regional Correctional Centre. With the help of Janet my co-worker, I continued the book's growth with "street stories" while I was on parole. I felt the responsibility of releasing these stories, poems, and drawings, to the world. So, I believed it was my calling from God, to do just that. An Aunt, now deceased, gave me some money, certainly enough to make photocopies of the original Connection to Freedom book.

Although I didn't understand the width and depth of it, I knew that on page 1 the author (myself) spoke about how Jesus Christ had saved me at the point of suicide in my cell, and I spoke about the book being a global ministry for Jesus Christ. Another book contributor was a man who had spent 23 years in prisons, and referred to how Jesus Christ saved his life, when he too was at the point of suicide; "Transformation of a Hollow man" is the title of his testimony.

So now that you have an idea of the book's contents, I will speak with you about the book's global outreach which was a single copy to a Toronto based TV ministry. An invitation to appear as a guest of the program was stopped by the guest co-coordinator due to seating problems. But the main man sent me a letter that said, about the Connection to Freedom book, "It is from the Lord".

Next, Janet and I went once again to mail a book, this was a suggestion by Don Baker, then minister with his wife Marg, at the Vancouver Island Regional Correctional Centre. The book was mailed one sunny afternoon to a prison in New South Wales in Australia. This was followed by single copy book donations to prisons and prison camps: Edmonton Remand Centre, in Alberta, The Pas Provincial Jail in Manitoba, Camp Chilliwack and Alouette River Unit in BC. There was not one response from any of those prisons or prison camps. I took several books to Vancouver Island Regional Correctional Centre for the schoolteacher, and gave a copy to the Salvation Army Corrections office.

I donated a copy each to John Howard Society of Victoria, Trinity Christian Centre, and the Victoria Public Library. Some weeks later I received a note from a library staff member to let me know their Connection to Freedom book, had been stolen. I received a letter from a church pastor in China, suggesting we send a copy of the Connection to Freedom book to help women addicted to morphine, who were at a recovery facility. Janet and I sent them a Connection to Freedom book. In a letter of response, they couldn't have expressed more gratitude.

A member of our Connection to Freedom group, who had spent time in a Texas prison implied that Texas inmates should read the book. Eventually I packaged up a book and mailed it to a Chaplain at the Texas Department of Corrections. His response almost made me weep for joy! He encouraged me and us to keep writing. A member of our Connection to Freedom meeting influenced me to send a book to where he had served time: Halifax Regional Correctional Centre. The Chaplain's response was "thank you for the Connection to Freedom book, on behalf of the inmates, the staff, and me".

The Connection to Freedom book became the Connection to Freedom Addictions Recovery Workbook, to the 2024, Workbook for Canadian and US inmates, Addicts, and Community groups.

Thanks to US Inmates

I remembered Ben and his wife Germaine, and their ministry at William Head Institution. I also recall how Germaine wrote me a letter from San Fransisco. She asked me to pray that God would open a door for her, and husband Ben, somewhere in California. She told me in follow up letters about her efforts at Mule Creek, Ironwood, and Eagle Mountain prisons. She was a Gospel singer, and Ben her husband, was a bible teacher, who would become a chaplain through the Mustard Seed Street Church, Victoria, BC, Canada.

Well, God opened a door for them when they moved to Blythe, California. Their ministry was to inmates at the California State Prison: Chuckwalla. Germaine was a Gospel singer there, and Ben taught inmates the word of God, using a Bible, and Bible based workbook. Ben and Germaine told the Christian inmate group about me and our Connection to Freedom meetings. Before you knew it, many years had passed, with the California inmates corresponding with our group, regularly. During this period, I had mailed my testimony to the Chuckwalla inmates which now follows:

At my worst I was a skid row alcoholic and dirty filthy junkie. Hospital staff, prison guards and my defense lawyer, decided I was worthless, and should be kept in jail after I broke into a drug store while suffering cold turkey withdrawal from narcotics. I had become addicted to morphine after a suicide attempt in California when I was 18 years old. By 24 years old I became a heroin addict. For the next 18 years off and on, I used heroin. When that "junk" was not available to me, I used opioid painkillers. When narcotics were not readily available, I committed crimes that would provide me with the price of "a fix", daily, for the next week.

When I met a girlfriend, also "a junkie", the cost became much higher. I became a dealer, and with a gang of ex-cons, I committed several crimes, burglaries, mostly. I was busted at a Pawn Shop with stolen goods. After that with two other guys, I was arrested on my way to rob a jewelry store. Whenever I could not connect with heroin, or narcotic pain killers, I used whiskey.

One night ready to "string myself up" in my cell, I found hope in Jesus Christ, and I was totally changed from a lost soul who only lived for drugs and alcohol satisfactions. With permission from my unit guard I walked around the jail, helping troubled inmates, and by phone their families. My fellow inmates helped me and between us we established the Connection to Freedom meetings for we inmates with alcohol and drug problems.

But, when security was threatened by the unusual inmate movement trying to get to our meetings, a 'Programs and Services' guard complained to me. "You can have the meetings in your unit, but we can't allow inmates from other units to attend! What is your decision, Bradley?" I answered: "If anybody in the jail is denied entry to our Connection to Freedom meeting, I will bring the meeting to an end!" So, the meeting came to an end, with a loud uproar from my unit. That's when I prayed in my cell, how we inmates could establish a program to help our recovery. God's answer to me was a program in the form of a book, titled, what else? Connection to Freedom book.

With the help of Janet, a volunteer from the community, I collected inmate stories and poems, and she did the typing at her home. When she brought the book back to the jail Janet had attached a note: "Well done you guys, keep up the good work!" Often, with the OK from the guards I sat with inmates, and as they told me about their life experiences, I did the writing. Before I left the prison on parole, I attended a Chapel service. The two ministers Don and Marg Baker asked me to stand up. On behalf of the inmates, whose signatures were recorded on a folded sheet of paper, I read, "Thanks, Steve, you and Connection to Freedom helped me", "Through God, you helped me, Steve". Not only inmates but one or two guards, and program persons, also signed their names. There were 36 signatures that proved to me **I have changed from the loser addict, drunk, I once was.**

On parole, through God's word, I was set free from my 4 packs a day cigarette addiction. Two years later at a Prayer Group led by Pastor Arthur Willis, at the Mustard Seed Street Church, Joanne, and Gordy, and others, and me, were told by Pastor Arthur: "I'm going to hand over this prayer stone and have you pass it on to each other. When the stone gets to each one of you, bow your head and ask God this question. "Is there anything in my life that You are not pleased with? If there is, please reveal that to me". When the stone reached me, and I prayed, and suddenly in my spirit was the word "Forgive!" Then as if watching a movie of my life, in my spirit, I flashed back to my childhood.

In my childhood, when I was eight or nine, I suffered debilitating asthma attacks. And being an introvert who was shy, didn't help me when it came to making school friends. The doctor had done every treatment that was possible, and always warned me about wearing a hat when it was raining, to avoid foggy days and to participate in breathing classes at the local hospital. Because of my breathing challenges I was unable to play sports with some neighborhood boys who were kicking a football. Embarrassed and feeling unworthy, as hard as anyone, I tried to run the length of the field. I had even found a discarded pair of boots and had them on when mom called across the field: "He's not like you boys my son is sickly! You better send him home now!" I was feeling worthless amid the laughter from some of my mates, so I went home. In my bedroom although I was brokenhearted, I refused to shed any tears.

One particularly cold and foggy morning when my asthma was close to being debilitating, I was at school when our class was given a surprising uplift. Our teacher's personal interpretation of some verses from her copy of the Holy Bible surprised me. This was not part of the school itinerary it was something she did on her own each day before classes. Our teacher was a gentle-spirited woman who reminded me of my soft-spoken grandma who I loved dearly. Imagining myself walking beside Bible characters, such as Paul the apostle, to me was refuge from the storms of my asthma attacks and reality. In fact, learning about the Bible was the driving force that I looked forward to every morning. I was inspired to attend Sunday school classes to learn more. Whether I was wheezing or having a good day I enjoyed listening to the Bible stories.

My daydreams were shattered one morning when at school some money went missing. Because the so called "victim" sat in front of me all the students' eyes were on my area. My breathing became labored, and I felt my cheeks turn red with embarrassment. I wanted to climb under my desk, but I was too afraid to even move. My shyness because of asthma saw me as the laughingstock for some pupils. I could not imagine any pain that was worse than being made to look like the class clown. But the grey haired, gentle spirited woman who was our teacher, pointed at me and in front of the class called me "thief!" My pain became worse, much worse. I had stolen nothing! But in that moment of sorrow, I felt deep resentment and walked away from God and any interest in her Bible, and I even quit Sunday school that until then I had attended every Sunday morning. I made a vow that I would never forgive my schoolteacher, and wanted nothing to do with God, Jesus, or The Holy Bible.

There in that Mustard Seed Street Church Prayer Group of 1990 I confessed my unforgiveness of 35 years for my childhood schoolteacher, with the Bible, who called me "thief!" And **I forgave her** there in Pastor Arthur's Prayer Group. No sooner had I forgiven when I felt as though a piano sized object was being lifted from my flesh. Instantly I recognized that God had released me from my addictions: alcohol, heroin, and other opioids. God's word two years previously had set me free from my 4 packs a day cigarette addiction.

To me it was a blessing and to Connection to Freedom members in attendance, to pick up the letters from my mail slot, and as a group share the letters from Corcoran, Chuckawalla, and Kern Valley state prisons, and a Massachusettes inmate. Collectively, we had shared correspondence with US inmates for 15 years.

If you want to change your life, the next page is your opportunity to do just that.

"What is salvation?"

It is impossible for us to find peace with God through our own efforts. Anything we try to do to obtain God's favor or gain salvation is worthless and futile. Salvation then, is a gift from God. He offers the gift through Jesus Christ, His son. By laying down His life on the cross, Jesus took our place and paid the ultimate price…death!

Salvation is by grace, through faith. There is nothing you did, or even can do, to deserve it! "For by grace you have been saved through faith, and that not of yourselves; it is the gift of God". (Ephesians 2:8)

If we do not know Jesus Christ, we have a problem. Our sin separates us from God, leaving us spiritually empty. "…for all have sinned and fall short of the glory of God". (Romans 3:23)

Jesus Christ is our only way to God, Jesus said, "I am the way, the truth, and the life. No one comes to the Father except through Me." (John 14:6) "But God demonstrates His own love toward us in that while we were still sinners, Christ died for us. (Romans 5:8). Receiving God's gift of salvation is not complicated. These steps 1-5 will explain.

(1) Admit you are a sinner and **Repent** of your sins, "Repent therefore and be converted that your sins may be blotted out, so that times of refreshing may come from the presence of the Lord." (Acts 3:19). A change of mind that results in a change of action. To repent then means to admit you are a sinner. You change your mind to agree with God that you are a sinner. The resulting change of action is, of course, the turning away from sin.

(2) Believe Jesus Christ died on the cross to save you from your sins and give you eternal life. "For God so loved the world that He gave His only begotten Son, that whoever believes in Him, should not perish but have everlasting life." (John 3:16) Believing in Jesus is also a part of repenting. You change your mind from unbelief to belief, which results in a change of action.

(3) Receive Jesus by faith. In John 14:6 Jesus said: I am the way, the truth, and the life. "No one comes to the Father except through Me." Faith in Jesus Christ is a change of mind that results in a change of action, i.e. receiving Him.

(4) You might **pray** a simple prayer to God **to thank Him** and make a simple spiritual connection.

(5) **Tell someone of the decision you have made and invite** that person to receive Jesus Christ. "And they overcame him by the blood of the Lamb and by the word of their testimony…" (Revelation 12:11). Remember, God's purpose for your life as a believer is to let the unsaved world know salvation for them is waiting. Say from God's word "If you confess with your mouth, the Lord Jesus and believe in your heart that God has raised Him from the dead, you will be saved. For with the heart one believes unto righteousness, and with the mouth confession is made unto salvation." (Romans 10:9-10)

Why I authored the book

I was addicted to cigarettes, alcohol, heroin, and other pain killers. My life's ambitions were to satisfy my criminal opportunities, in support of my addictions. Jail cells, the psych ward, and suicide attempts in California, and Victoria, BC was my life. I smashed a glass door to a drug store, and broke in and five years later, I was charged with attempted robbery of another drug store.

In 1987, I was an inmate at the Vancouver Island Regional Correctional Centre. I hit rock bottom in my addictions and found Jesus Christ. My whole being was transformed from an angry, self-absorbed man wheeling and dealing drugs, to a person of peace, with love for his fellow man. I helped inmates with their problems, and with their participation, and help, established the Connection to Freedom meetings, and with the assistance of a community member, and some encouragement by correctional staff, and chaplaincy, the Connection to Freedom book.

While on parole, through prayer and the word of God, on the 16th of February 1988, I was set free from my four pack a day cigarette addiction. Two years after my parole finished, 1990, although I didn't want to go at first, I attended a Prayer Group, led by Rev Arthur Willis. He told the group: "Tonight, we are going to ask the Lord if there's anything He is not pleased with in our lives and to reveal it to each one of us. During that day I had been struggling with thoughts of alcohol, and heroin, that's why I didn't want to attend the Prayer Group.

With my head bowed I prayed for God to reveal those things in my life He was not pleased with. Instantly I saw in my spirit, "Forgive" and just as quickly I realized this was about a person for whom I had held unforgiveness for 35 years. I stood up, and confessed my unforgiveness, and from my heart, I repented and forgave that person. Never will I forget the power of forgiveness because that night I felt as if the Lord was removing a piano sized object from my flesh. I knew that He was removing my addiction to alcohol, heroin, pain killers, from my life.

With today's date being Feb 25, 2024, since 1988, and 1990 when God through prayer, and His word, released me from my addictions to cigarettes, alcohol, heroin, and pain killers, not once have I returned to these substances. However, a broken relationship almost caused me to relapse, but God was there for me, in His word, and I didn't relapse. Recovery for me is as the bible says, 'one day at a time'.

The reason I authored this book, with testimonials from friends, is to help inmates, and addicts, and community groups such as churches, or locally, recovery groups nationwide in Canada, and in the USA. As you will see in the workbook Jesus Christ and God's word is the key that unlocks the pain of addiction, and unforgiveness. My life ministry for the Lord was and is, Mark 11:25-26 which taught, and continues to teach me, to forgive.

The exercises were not lightly submitted. Inmates locally, Canada wide, and throughout the USA, via many years of correspondence, gave me suggestions, but for the most part, they challenged and met my own needs for recovery and rehabilitation through Christ. Truly, the three words that God spoke to me in jail, totally changed my life, "Help these men". God gave me a further blessing, some who have contributed their stories, as do I, speak about helping 'youth at risk' which is a benefit to any community in Canada and the US.

Acknowledgments

Doug and Jane for their prayers and encouragement through many years, and Katie, Bart, and Gloria for their prayers and help. Mark and Teresa for their kindness and encouragement. Syd for sharing his story with me and listening to mine. Tejuanis "Butch" Cassidy and wife, Donna, for their friendship. Shirley who "lives the Gospel," Reima-Lee, (all the best in Quesnel Sis) and Pastor Aneil of Connection to Freedom Community Church for his regular telephone calls, and to Sue, his mother, for her warrior prayers, Alberto, and family, God bless you and to Janet Johnson for her work formatting the Connection to Freedom book, and her present work with seniors. Thank you to Jesse, and Hannah for your words of encouragement.

Kurt and Pat for their prayers and encouragement over the years, Joseph, once deacon at the Chinese Pentecostal Church. Wendy, videographer, and friend, for her video re: work-book introduction. Thanks also to Mary for her contribution, and Lesley for her Seniors meal assistance. My mother who twice volunteered and served dinners at the Needle Exchange, passed away in 2022 and is greatly missed by her family.

Joel, Micki, and daughters, who twice assisted with Needle Exchange meal distribution. University of Victoria students who also helped. Thanks also to Kerri, and her two daughters for helping at the Needle Exchange.

Former Connection to Freedom board president, Ross Pomeroy, a dear friend who was often a mentor to me; he has gone to be with the Lord. Board member Gary who was regularly our transportation, and board member Gaston, a gardener with many talents. Thank you to Reverend Alanna Menu of Centennial United Church for Gaston's Celebration of Life service. Board member Greg, my friend who was my co-speaker at Victoria high schools, Parkland Secondary School, particularly. Thank you to Lorne Chan for his hospitality as a teacher. Likewise, the Camosun College Criminal Justice classes, and instructors. Thanks to Garey for his testimony at the college and for this workbook.

Those who attended Connection to Freedom meetings and have since passed: a certain mental illness drove "AJ" to end his own life. Thanks to his family who showed true humility and character that gave me, and us, a measure of calm when it was so badly needed. We remember Trent, a young man gone too soon, and Joe, whose mother Kellie, we pray for. In memory of Rev Chris and with assurance of our prayers for Dianne.

My longtime California friend, Robert Price of KGET TV Bakersfield. His news item on toxic drugs was extremely helpful. To Kerri, Billy, Glenn, and Janet, for their artistic contributions, and to all those whose stories gave this workbook purpose. My appreciation to all guest speakers and to actor/ director Michael Farrell, not only as my co-speaker, and friend but for his inspiration and encouragement for me to reach out to actors. Thanks to Vicky (wonderful singer) and hello to Jim.

There were also those who encouraged me with the words "Keep up the good work" and that was Catherine Urquhart of BCTV, now with Global News Vancouver. Her coverage of Vancouver Island Regional Correctional Centre, and Bev's and my work, in the meeting room at Manchester House, was greatly appreciated. Thanks, Bev Walmsley.

"Obie" your story from the Connection to Freedom book, and your assistance with our school talks, especially, the Claremont Secondary School, was indeed a blessing to the teachers, fellow speakers, and me. Keep up the good work! Al, many thanks for your story, and Chuck, the same with you, my friend. Remembering my friend, former journalist, Gordon Pollard.

To Sybil, who gave input to my seminar on youth violence that was held in the gym at Centennial United Church. Dr. Jack, Reima-Lee, and the Salvation Army input, along with Greg, and the woman in recovery. I appreciate all your opinions and ideas. Thanks Don and Marg Baker.

My brother Phill passed away recently. Sorry for your loss Duane, Tina, and Braden, I have placed two poems in this book to tell Phill's story. One is titled "Trucker", and the other is about his dog.

To those media who helped us get the message of hope out to those in the community of Greater Victoria, and beyond. *Radio:* CKDA, CJVI, CFUV, CKMO, CBC Radio One. *TV:* Chek TV, Shaw Community TV, BCTV. *Newspapers:* Times-Colonist, Peninsula News, Victoria News, Saanich News, News Group. *Newsmagazine:* Education Leader. *Telephone interview:* with Robert Price then with 'The Bakersfield Californian' newspaper.

I wish to thank Dr. F. Edora, and Marie, Dr. Wallace, and BC Ambulance Service, Royal Jubilee Hospital, Victoria General Hospital, and the two Hep C, nurses who made my treatment a gentle challenge, and successful. Thanks also to the doctor overseeing my case.

As part of my Dedication to this book, I have referred to a U.S. doctor who saved my life. The name of that physician is Dr. Robert Hamblin of the Ridgecrest Community Hospital, in California. As he is no longer with us, RIP, I thank his sons. One of whom I believe lives in Hawaii.

Canadian and U.S. correspondence: My thanks for the letters from Fraser Regional Correctional Centre, William Head Institution, Mission Institution, Kent Institution, Prince George Regional Correctional Centre, Matsqui Institution, Saskatchewan Penitentiary, Halifax Regional Correctional Centre, Dorchester Penitentiary, Texas Department of Corrections, Corcoran State Prison, Chuckwalla State Prison, Kern Valley State Prison, San Quentin, and South Dakota State Penitentiary, and five years of letters from an inmate in Massachusetts.

Chaplain Fran, Ben and Germaine, Peter Forbes, Allan and Gloria, and Rev Alanna Menu of Centennial United Church.

Thanks to the staff and students of the Lauwelnew Tribal School for the handmade 'Thank you cards' for my eight-week Life Skills program. And to Pacific Christian School for the several years inviting our talks. Thanks also to Ian Lam, Royal Jubilee Dental Clinic, for his warm comments after reading one of my books. Thanks Sandy for your poem.

Thank you, Corrine, for your encouragement, and to all Chown residents, and workers who motivated me, and inspired me, to continue writing. Thank you, Terry P, for your assistance. Likewise, to Art, Rae, Pauline, and Dawn. To Mr. Larsen, and Mr. Christiansen. Thank you for your support: John Howard Society of Victoria, the Methadone Clinic, Aids Vancouver Island, Salvation Army ARC, Our Place, Vancouver Island Regional Correctional Centre, and the South Island Counselling and Training Centre which made a difference in my life. My thanks to the Immigration Lawyer who expressed his concern for the homeless, of Pandora Avenue. Thanks for your good thoughts Erna, and finally, Thank you Paul, Jeff, Billy, and Athena. Thanks to T. Kennedy, and to the Sparrow family, Cindy (CP), Gerry R, Ken H, thanks to Mike, Gerald, and Madeleine. Thank you Wendy (CP).

And to the family of the First Nations grandmother, and grandson David (last name not revealed but I remember it) who saved my life, at Stave Lake, BC.

I am grateful to Alcoholics Anonymous and Narcotics Anonymous, for the help I received. And to Andy, whose 12 Steps seminar, at the VIRCC, gave me information that helped save my life. My God as I understand Him is Jesus Christ.

I am grateful to the New King James Bible for the guiding light the words provided. Thank you David, Divina, Ted, Irene, K. Trussler, Dr. Jack.

Thank you to Tejuanis "Butch" Cassidy and wife Donna, for their support and encouragement. Many thanks Mr. and Mrs Gareth Evans.

If you attended even one Connection to Freedom meeting, and/ or contributed a story, poem, or drawing to the Connection to Freedom book, and/ or where my co-speaker either in church, or school, or college criminal justice class, you are part of the ministry that led to this workbook. For which I thank all the churches and ministries who are mentioned throughout the workbook. See: The Needle Exchange (page 60-61).

Attention: Should you wish to write a letter to the author, or to any of the contributing writers, or artists, or anything to do with the workbook, send your letter, to: Steve Bradley, Connection to Freedom Society, #1-5201 Trans Canada Highway, Duncan, BC, V9L 6W3. Make sure in your letter you say which person you are writing to.

Remember to put Canada in your address if you are writing from the USA. Please make sure your return address is on the envelope. Thank you. If you enjoy poetry, Steve Bradley has a book of poems, God willing, soon to be released.

Printed in the USA
CPSIA information can be obtained
at www.ICGtesting.com
JSHW010443081124
73092JS00004B/6